Christ The Cornerstone

"Building the Kingdom in a Changing World"

Susan Blum Gerding

Available from:
Jeremiah Press
5840 Wind Drift Lane
Boca Raton, Florida 33433
Jeremiahpr@aol.com

ISBN Number: 1-883520-21-5

Copyright © 2002. Susan Blum Gerding.
All rights reserved.

Jeremiah Press
Boca Raton, Florida
Printed in the United States of America

Table of Contents

Introduction *vii*

Chapter One
    Stress, Crisis, and Trauma   *1*

Chapter Two
    Naming Our Fears/Owning Our Losses   *25*

Chapter Three
    Unforgiveness—A Major Stumbling Block   *47*

Chapter Four
    We Call on God's Healing   *67*

Chapter Five
    Instruments of Change   *97*

Appendix A
    Revised Holmes Rahe Scales   *127*

Appendix B
    Facilitator's Guide for Weekly Meetings   *130*

Appendix C
    Common Reactions to Stress?
    Is Stress Always Bad for You?
    Signs of Stress Overload   *131*

Appendix D
    Reactions to Severe Crisis   *133*

Appendix E
    Acute Trauma Reaction
    Trauma "Do's" and "Don't's"   *134*

Appendix F
    Rebuilding the Church:
    A Call to Personal Holiness   *138*

Appendix G
    Group Guidelines for Discussion   *144*

About the Author

Dr. Susan Blum Gerding has been actively proclaiming the Good News through a variety of communication styles and methods since 1979. She received her master's degree in Pastoral Ministry from St. Thomas University, Miami, and her doctorate in Adult Education/Leadership Development at Florida Atlantic University, one of the thirteen universities in the Florida state system.

Dr. Gerding, a convert, was the founding editor of *The Catholic Evangelist* magazine and has written a total of nine books and evangelization training manuals, including the 1993 *Text, Study, Guide, and Implementation Process for Go and Make Disciples* developed in consultation with the NCCB Committee on Evangelization.

Her most recent work, *Lay Ministers, Lay Disciples: Evangelizing Power in the Parish* (Paulist Press, 1999*)*, was co-authored with Rev. Frank DeSiano, CSP.

Dr. Gerding is the president of Isaiah Ministries, which has offered a model of clergy/lay preaching teams and local parish involvement in more than 1200 Isaiah Parish Missions throughout the United States, Canada, and Europe.

A popular speaker at national, diocesan, and parish conferences throughout the U.S., she is also the president of Jeremiah Press, which specializes in publishing books on Catholic spirituality.

In 1984, she was given the *Pro Ecclesia et Pontifice* Medal by Pope John Paul II, and in 1996 received the "Pope Paul VI Award for Leadership in Catholic Evangelization," given by the National Council for Catholic Evangelization.

She lives with her husband Ed in Boca Raton, Florida, where they are active members of St. Jude Church. Together, they are the parents of ten children and thirteen grandchildren.

DEDICATION

For my children and grandchildren, new generations of builders

"May those who come behind us find us faithful."

ACKNOWLEDGMENTS

My deepest appreciation goes to the nineteen Isaiah preachers, especially Father Dennis Chriszt, CPPS, Father Jim McKarns, and Gerry Downs, D. Min., who provided input into the process and content of the parish mission, "Building the Kingdom in a Changing World." Special thanks go to Father John Graden, OSFS, and Father Ray Kellarman for their especially helpful critiques of the earlier work.

As this book progressed as a resource for the mission, I am greatly indebted to Janice Valvano for her precise and constructive editing, to Norene Dupre for her most helpful suggestions, and to Dr. Catherine Dower Gold for her meticulous proofreading.

This book could not have been written without the patience and support of my dear husband, Ed. Many thanks to all.

Other Books*
by
Susan Blum Gerding

Mission: Evangelization Training Manual
The Ministry of Evangelization
(Liturgical Press)
Renew Your Faith
Faith in Action
Share Your Faith Training Manual
"Implementation Process for 'Go and Make Disciples'"
Heart to Heart Evangelization Training
Lay Minister, Lay Disciples:
Evangelizing Power in the Parish
(Paulist Press)

*Available at Jeremiah Press, unless otherwise noted.

Introduction

Compounded Stress

Since the beginning of the 21st Century, stress levels have escalated rapidly. For decades, the 1967 Holmes Rahe *Social Readjustment Rating Scale* was widely used to determine how much stress we could experience in one year before we were likely to fall ill to a serious health condition. Forty years ago, the top ten stressful life events and their values were:

1. Death of spouse—100
2. Divorce—73
3. Marital separation—65
4. Jail term—63
5. Death of close family member—63
6. Personal injury or illness—53
7. Marriage—50
8. Fired at work—47
9. Marital reconciliation—45
10. Retirement—45

The 1967 list was revised in 2000, naming the same ten items as most serious.[1] Neither list names items such as drug and alcohol abuse, spousal abuse, abortion, single parenting, death of a child, kidnapping of a child, road rage, adult children returning home, caring for aging parents, tattoos or body-piercing—let alone terrorist attacks!

Prior to September 11, 2001, Americans experienced stressful situations daily, and these problems, tragedies, and common losses still occur. Now, the common stress of daily life is additionally compounded by the unprecedented combined stress of three major crises which

---

[1] Please see Appendix A for the revised lists for adults and children.

occurred within less than a year in America. At this writing, it is now 15 months after the horrendous September 11, 2001, terrorist attacks. It is less than a year after the sexual abuse scandal in the Catholic Church broke wide open in Boston in January 2002. It is less than six months after the corporate fraud scandals resulting in economic chaos surfaced in May 2002. Life goes on, after these three particular events—the terrorist attacks, the sexual abuse scandal in the Church, and the economic crisis—but not without new levels of stress and future crises, as well.

Unsurpassable Opportunity

In light of these three major crises (and crises yet to come), the Church in America has been presented with an unsurpassable opportunity. The 19,000-plus parishes in the United States could be a major source of comfort, reconciliation, healing, and courage in the face of these crises.

Many of us find ourselves coping to one degree or another with the direct or indirect results of these three crises, while still struggling with the ordinary distress of life events.

For many Americans, these disasters and scandals have brought an end to a decades-long period of trust, well-being, security, and safety. Now, for many, fear and crisis go hand in hand with scandal and distrust. Experts in all three fields—terrorism, sexual abuse, and corporate collapse—predict that we have seen only the tip of the iceberg. Predictions for the future are clear: these problems simply cannot and will not be "wished" away!

For all of these reasons, we have developed a new Isaiah Parish Mission, *Building the Kingdom in a Changing World*, to address these issues. This book, *Christ the Cornerstone*, serves as the accompanying adult religious education component for the mission. It is designed to support the new mission, both as a pre-mission guide for the local mission team and as a post-mission follow-up resource for the entire parish.[2] While this book was written specifically as a companion text to support the new mission format, it also stands alone for individual study and reflection. In other words, you do not need to participate in the mission to gain the benefits suggested in this book.

Christ, the Cornerstone

At World Youth Day in Toronto on July 27, 2002, Pope John Paul II addressed the terror and damage done on September 11. He summarized his feelings, stating:

"The question that arises is dramatic and will not go away: On what foundations, on what certainties, should we build our lives and the life of the community to which we belong?

"A new generation of builders is needed. Moved not by fear, or violence, but by the urgency of genuine love, they must learn to build, brick by brick, the city of God . . . Christ alone is the cornerstone on which it is possible to solidly build one's existence."

Our challenge is to rebuild the kingdom in our ever-changing world. For Christians, the very roots of safety and security have been uprooted and shaken—but not crushed or destroyed. While terror may surround us, we must remember that our faith is built on a strong foundation. For those whose faith has been shaken, we must remember that we are living stones built upon a rock, a cornerstone, strong and secure and unshakeable—the cornerstone of Jesus Christ.

---

[2] Please see Appendix B for suggested uses of this manual.

New Parish Mission

Building the Kingdom in a Changing World is a four-night parish mission which is specifically designed to offer parish leadership a tool which focuses on helping people cope with 21st Century stress.

This mission is centered on Christ the cornerstone as the only secure foundation on which we can build our lives. The goals are the same for both the mission and this book:

1) to help congregations and individuals make sense of a world of chaos and confusion, without attempting to analyze, assign blame, or fix any of these crises;

2) to help parish leadership assist parishioners in coping with various crises affecting their lives and the lives of their loved ones, whatever the crises might be, whatever the degree of pain might be, and whatever new crises might arise;

3) to foster an understanding and perspective which will help to alleviate or neutralize *unnecessary* fear, anxiety, guilt, or anger;

4) to provide a spiritual aid to help people deal with the events of the times within a sound psychological, theological, and pastoral context;

5) to invite people to a deeper, more intimate relationship with Jesus Christ, the cornerstone of our lives.

The foundational scripture verse for both the mission and the book is *Isaiah* 28:16:

> *See, I am laying a stone in Zion, a stone that has been tested. A precious cornerstone as a sure foundation; he who puts faith in it shall not be shaken.*

Purpose and Structure of Book

The basic purpose of this book is to help us cope with additional stressful events. Therefore, it is designed specifically to accomplish the following:

1) **to enable** us to be less fearful/angry/guilty
2) **to encourage** us to be more loving, caring, and sensitive to others
3) **to empower** us to be more knowledgeable about our options to overcome a sense of powerlessness
4) **to establish** a sense of joy and hope, so we all will enjoy life more, without fear and anxiety as principle conditions of life
5) **to encounter** and recognize the blessings which result from various crises in our lives

There is much story-telling and personal experience in all of the chapters. Chapter One serves primarily as an introductory chapter, providing many facts concerning the definition and management of stress, crisis, and trauma. The remaining four chapters are structured around the themes of the four nightly mission sessions. Also, the Appendixes offer more detailed information for additional understanding.

Each chapter integrates pastoral, psychological, practical, and prayerful suggestions for coping within a context of sound theology and adult education principles. One of the most important adult education principles is that the material learned must be able to be applied immediately. To fulfill this requirement, quotations and scriptural passages are included at the end of each chapter in the "Food for Thought" section, as well as questions to facilitate reflection, discussion, prayer, and action.

Skyrocketing Stress

Another very important principle of adult education is that the topic must be relevant. We have all been touched by the major crises. No one is exempt—not the "Greatest Generation" (WW II folks), nor the Baby Boomers, Generation X, or Generation Y. All age cohorts have been affected one way or another.

A CBS-*New York Times* poll released just a few days prior to the 2002 midterm elections said that the economy clearly was the top issue on voters' minds. And "anxieties about the possibility of another terrorist attack in the next few months remain high, with 75% saying such an attack is likely."[3]

"A host of new studies show that stress in the workplace is skyrocketing," reports Cora Daniels in her article entitled 'The Last Taboo' in *Fortune Magazine*.[4] She interviewed dozens of stress experts such as MDs, psychiatrists, therapists, and workplace gurus. She concludes, "Blame it on the economy, terrorism, the new 24/7 workweek, corporate scandals—whatever the cause, stress levels are at record highs."

Dr. Stephen Schoonover, head of an executive development firm which helps executives combat stress and balance their lives, reports, "I have seen **my practice surge 30% over the past two years.** People are absolutely nuts, stressed off the map," Shoonover says. "I've never seen it this bad."[5]

Stress management expert Ellen Dunn, Ph.D., reports that recent research shows that these days Americans are more stressed than ever; most of us are experiencing **at least 15% more stress on a daily basis** than we did just three years ago. Dunn explains the upsurge, "Studies show

---

[3] CBS-*New York Times* poll released November 2, 2002, reported on AOL News, November 3, 2002.

[4] Cora Daniels, "The Last Taboo," *Fortune Magazine*, 10/28/2002

[5] Daniels, op cit.

it's partly due to the fact that as a society, we're watching and reading more news than we used to. A recent survey shows viewer-ship of TV news programs is soaring . . . and even though events at the other end of the world may not affect us directly, research shows just hearing about it makes us feel stressed."[6]

Fallout

People's concerns come from multiple sources. Let's look briefly at three main sources.

1) Terrorism. In addition to expecting future terrorist attacks, biochemical warfare was initiated as a real threat with the introduction of anthrax. Homeland Security became a major priority, with its resultant military police armed with machine guns and automatic weapons scanning the airport crowds. Hearts are pounding with "dirty bombs," "mailbox bombs," and gas mask anxieties. War looms on the horizon as a distinct possibility.

2. Sexual abuse in the Church. Additionally, the horrendous scandal of sexual abuse of minors in the Catholic Church has resulted in several hundred priests and several bishops resigning in disgrace. Criminal charges are still pending against some, while others have been convicted and are presently serving prison terms.

A crisis of trust has arisen for many Catholics who do not know if they can trust the bishops who appear to have participated in a conspiracy of silence, looking the other way and transferring abusive priests from parish to parish. Like the September 11 tragedy, the Church crisis elicited fear, anger, and distrust.

Fortunately, many Catholics regained some confidence in the bishops after the passage of the "zero toler-

---

[6] Ellen Dunn, "Stress Breakthroughs," *Woman's World*, September 17, 2002, 14-15

ance" agreement in Dallas in June 2002. Then, six months later at the November meeting of the bishops, the agreement was modified, according to Rome's guidelines in such a way as to protect the innocent and to hold accountable the guilty.

On the whole, Americans' confidence in institutional religion reached its lowest point in thirty years, according to a July 2002 Gallup Poll. Only 45 percent of Americans have a "great deal or quite a lot" of confidence in the church or organized religion, down from sixty percent last year and the lowest since Gallup started collecting the data in 1973. The previous low point for religion came in 1989, at 52 percent, when Protestants were rocked by televangelist scandals involving sex, money, and public falls from grace. Not surprisingly, today Catholics have less faith in institutional religion (42 percent) compared to 59 percent of Protestants. In 1991, ratings by Catholics and Protestants were relatively the same.[7]

3) Economic collapse. The third crisis, the crumbling of many economic and government institutions, brought the stock market tumbling to a five-year low, with the departure of 44 chief executive officers in just the first 11 days of June 2002, in addition to 80 CEO departures in May. In July, WorldCom, the nation's second-largest long-distance carrier, joined the ranks of Enron, Tyco, Merrill Lynch and Arthur Anderson, among others, accused of corporate fraud. WorldCom had overstated its cash flow by $3.8 billion, which resulted in the immediate firing of 17,000 employees. Bankruptcy papers have been filed. Who knows what will come from that? It's not clear how a bankruptcy filing would affect the millions of consumers and thousands of large companies that use WorldCom's voice and data services. WorldCom also is the world's largest carrier of Internet traffic.

---

[7] *National Catholic Reporter,* July, 2002, p.8.

Investor distrust across the board is at an all-time high, with a drop of nearly 700 points on September 17, 2001, the first trading day after September 11 and nearly 400 points in mid-July 2002 to bring the market below 8,000, its lowest point since October 1998.

Institutions are disintegrating like 401(k) s. People are losing their life-savings or their children's education funds. Trusted institutions like the FBI, CIA, banks, and corporations are in question. Even Martha Stewart and the Red Cross are suspect.

Every group across the board economically is feeling the fallout of the economic crisis, including the poor and the homeless. According to an annual survey by the Association of Gospel Rescue Missions, almost 60percent of the 20,000 homeless people surveyed nationally in October 2002 said it was more difficult for them to find work than it was six months ago. Families consisting of a husband, wife, and children accounted for 25 percent of families served, an increase from 17 percent in 2001 and the largest percentage ever for that group in the survey's 14 year history. The association also found that *33 percent of those surveyed had never been homeless before.*[8]

Making Sense Out of a World of Chaos

It is my fervent hope and prayer that American Catholics and the leadership of our churches will find this book (and the mission, if they choose to offer it to their congregations) spiritual, practical, down-to-earth, and helpful tools. In such a rapidly changing world, it is understood that the specific current events will change, but the scriptural, psychological, and educational principles of this book

---

[8] "Survey says most homeless find it harder to get work," *National Catholic Reporter*, November 22, 2002, (emphasis mine) page 10.
Note: The Association of Gospel Rescue Missions represents 302 rescue missions that provide emergency food, shelter and other services to families, recovering addicts, the elderly and at-risk youth.

will still stand as we rebuild the Church and the World with Jesus Christ as *our* cornerstone.

May God bless the many, many people who will be aided in making sense out of a world of chaos and confusion; in reconciling their fear and anxiety; in renewing and strengthening their faith in our loving, compassionate God; and in recommitting their lives and service as disciples of Jesus Christ in the power of the Holy Spirit.

With tremendous gratitude to God for the mercy, goodness, and generosity we all still experience in this rapidly changing, chaotic, splendor-filled world . . .

Gratefully,

Susan Blum Gerding
November 28, 2002
Thanksgiving Day

CHAPTER ONE

STRESS, CRISIS AND TRAUMA

"The world breaks everyone and afterward many are strong at the broken places."
Ernest Hemingway

Opening Prayer

God Our Father, so much of our world appears to have fallen apart—national security, financial security, institutional distrust, global warfare, and unrest. Help us to understand the stress with which we find ourselves dealing. Be with us on the journey as we attempt to find joy and peace in place of the fear, anxiety, and confusion which many of us now feel. Strengthen our faith and trust in you. We ask all of this in Jesus' Most Holy Name. Amen.

Stress, Crisis, and Trauma – What's the Difference?

Definition: *Stress* (distress) is a state of being in pain, suffering, affliction; a state of danger or trouble. Distress implies mental or physical strain imposed by pain, trouble, worry, or the like and usually suggests a state or situation that can be relieved. Stress includes three stages: 1) alarm, 2) resistance or adaptation, and 3) exhaustion.

Definition: *Crisis* is stress, magnified a hundred times. A synonym for crisis is *emergency*, a time of great danger or trouble, whose outcome decides whether very serious, negative consequences will follow.

Definition: *Trauma* is defined as a severe, sudden, and inescapable event which carries the actual or implicit threat of death or personal injury. Similar to a crisis, a traumatic event is much more overwhelming and so critically stressful that our ability to cope, or even to function at all is at risk.

The difference between stress, crisis, and trauma might be described as a matter of degree. For example:

Stress: final exams, a toothache, or severe thunder storms
Crisis: academic probation, a severe dental abscess, or hurricane warnings
Trauma: expulsion from college, heart failure during extraction of the tooth, actual landfall of a Stage Five hurricane

Stress is usually not a life or death situation unless, of course, it is prolonged and unrelieved (distress). Crisis and trauma may both be regarded as severe, unexpected emergency situations varying in degree, circumstances, and the people involved. For instance, the Church sexual abuse scandal was viewed by most Catholics, priests and laity alike, as a crisis. However, it was traumatic for the victims, and, it well may have reached traumatic proportions for some of the bishops and priests involved. The same could be said of the varying degrees of the corporate fraud scandals which resulted in stress, crisis, and trauma depending on a person's involvement.

Stress

First, let us examine the condition known as stress. How many of you, since September 11, 2001, have been sick, injured, or lost your job? How many have had surgery, had a baby, lost a spouse? How many were married, were divorced, or retired? All of these, plus a myriad of other situations, including going on vacation, celebrating holidays, or receiving a significant award, are life-changing events which cause stress.

Case: Jane is a single mom, working as a supervisor of a credit card company, raising a twelve-year-old son whose father has never been a part of their life. Faced with increases in rent and groceries and struggling just to make ends meet, she took on a second job on the weekends—just to "get by." Her son, Johnny, is in the sixth grade, doing well in school and sports, but he missed Mom on the weekends. She was always tired and simply could not afford more than a few dollars a week for his allowance.

One Saturday night, she found out that he and some of his friends at Skate Board Kingdom, their hangout, had picked the locks of some vending machines. A visit from the local police with Johnny in tow was enough to scare the daylights out of Johnny—and Jane, too! Johnny was soon in trouble again, though, this time for experimenting with drugs. Marijuana. Jane was frightened and sought counseling, which she found on a sliding scale fee basis at the community center. She quit her weekend job to be more available to her son. Johnny continued to hang out with the wrong crowd and eventually became mired down in juvenile court for petty theft.

And then came September 11!

Case: Lou and his wife, Sarah, retired to South Florida two years ago after working at a major telecommunications company ever since it was founded during the '80s. Many bonuses had been paid in stock options, and Lou and Sarah found themselves very comfortable by the time he took an early retirement at the age of 55. They joined a local country club, played golf, visited with their children and grandchildren, traveled to Europe, and loved their retirement.

Then came September 11, which they survived fairly well, except that they vowed never to fly again which eliminated many of their visits with families and most of their vacations. If they couldn't drive, they wouldn't go. Adjustments were made, but one thing Lou noticed was that the stock market, after taking an initial dive and recovering, was going down a little at a time, and then would shoot back up, and then come down a little more.

And then came May 8, 2002. Lou had worked for WorldCom. His stock which had been valued at an all-time high of $62 per share only a year earlier was now worth six cents a share!

Case: Nancy is a widow and was struggling along with everyone else over the national security issues after the terrorist attacks on September 11. A devout Catholic and very, very active in the Church all her life, she was stunned when the clergy crisis raised its ugly head in Boston in January 2002. As the scandal mounted and spread all over the United States, leaving virtually no diocese untouched, she became enraged and frustrated.

She approached her pastor, asking him for permission to form a small lay leadership group which at least could discuss the problem and try to find some ways for their fellow parishioners to deal with that issue.

The pastor did not say, "No," nor did he say "Yes!" He simply chose not to respond, saying, "I'll get back to you" and, of course, never did.

All attempts at dialogue with her parish priests were ignored. She felt useless and worthless. When she went to Mass, she found herself crying. She felt entirely powerless. There was not a thing she could do other than write letters of support and encouragement to her many, many priest

.and bishop friends. Eventually, this former daily communicant quit going to Mass altogether. It simply was too painful. Normally a "mover and shaker" in her parish, she was not used to being "stonewalled."

Finally, she discovered a lay group (Voice of the Faithful) which had formed in the Boston area, contacted them, and attended a July rally where she joined 4,200 other Catholics from 40 states who had similar feelings. She felt very comfortable with their centrist point of view, neither promoting ordination of women and a married priesthood on one side nor a strictly traditionalist, hierarchical approach on the other. When she returned home, she was discredited and undermined in her attempts to form a local chapter of this group.

Before her retirement, Nancy had worked for the Church as a social worker with Catholic Charities. She lived on her meager social security monthly allotment, plus a small inheritance of stocks and bonds, left to her by her father. Now there was practically nothing left!

Case: John and Joann, both highly educated, multi-disciplined engineers holding MBAs, had been married for seven years and were working in the booming energy field headquartered in Houston. They finally had saved enough for a down payment on a new home and were happily living in the suburbs with their five-year-old son. Even with the added cost of kindergarten tuition for Peter at the local Catholic school, they were able to make ends meet and even were able to save a little each month for a vacation.

And then came the downfall of Enron. Both lost their jobs and found it difficult to find employment since there were so many other young, talented engineers in the same situation. After several months of job-seeking, John eventually found another position but with a much lower income; Joann ended up as a helper in the school cafeteria! The stock options they had frequently been awarded as bonuses at Enron were worthless. They were living from paycheck to paycheck.

All of these stories are true. Of course, the names have been changed for the sake of confidentiality, but all of these *real* people have been struggling with multi-leveled *real* stress, just as millions of Americans are today.

Long-Term Stress

Case: Claudia and Sam live a few blocks away from me. In early September 2001 Sam lost his job after serving as a town engineer for over seventeen years. And then came September 11. After many weeks of seeking a new position, Sam finally found one shortly before Christmas.

In January, his older brother died of a massive heart attack at the age of 51. In February, Claudia was let go from her position, as a result of downsizing.

One month later, in March, she was diagnosed with breast cancer and in April had a double mastectomy. In May she began a six-month protocol of chemotherapy and radiation and had her first dose of chemo, which made her deathly ill for three days.

The very same day she began the chemotherapy, her father, in his early sixties, had open heart surgery and, according to his surgeon, "was doing fine, would be sent home in a few days, and would live for another twenty years." However, during the third night after surgery, complications arose and he suffocated in his sleep.

Three months after starting the chemotherapy, Claudia was told that she would have to have a hysterectomy. And throughout all of this, Claudia and Sam were raising a teenaged daughter who had just turned sixteen. Normally, she was a very level-headed teenager with good grades and a part-time job at the local grocery store. While Claudia and Sam now have the added stress of helping her deal with her mother's illness, they also must face the disappointing fact that their college savings fund for her has nearly been wiped out. The daughter is angry and confused. Sam suffers anxiety and worries about finances, as well as his wife's recuperation. Claudia is depressed and suicidal.

True story. Long term, multi-leveled stress.

What Causes Stress?

Three potential sources for stress are 1) specific events, 2) the general conditions in our lives, and 3) our belief systems.

Events, big or small, can cause acute stress, depending on our perception of the event, our ability to withstand stress, and the amount of stress already present in our lives.

The *general conditions in our lives* such as our physical health, emotional state, relationships, surroundings, or jobs can cause chronic stress. These conditions are stressful in and of themselves, but they also make it harder to handle other pressures or demands in our lives. (The stressful nature of these general conditions has been intensified for nearly everyone due to the three major crises. Add normal life events to these intensified general conditions, and our stress can become overwhelming.)

Our *belief system* (our perceptions about the world, life, ourselves, and what's important in life) can contribute to our stress level when our lives do not seem to live up to our values or expectations. (For Catholics, the church crisis particularly affects this area of stress-inducing causes.)

How Much Stress Can a Person Take?

In the late sixties a scale was developed by two psychologists, T. H. Holmes and R. H. Rahe, to measure stress levels due to recent life events. This scale, which was previously mentioned in the Introduction is known as the Holmes-Rahe *Social Readjustment Rating Scale* and was widely used for decades to determine how much stress a person could experience. Forty-three life-changing items were listed, from "death of a spouse" at the top of the list valued at 100 points to "minor violations of the law" at the bottom of the list with only eleven points assigned. Both positive and negative life events were listed, including "outstanding personal achievement," "marriage," "vacation," and "Christmas."

Depending on how many life events a person experienced in a twelve month period and the total points accumulated, the probability of a serious health change could be predicted. Three hundred or more points equaled a 50 – 90 percent chance of serious health change. More than 450 points predicted a 90 % chance of serious health problems.

Viewing that scale now, from the vantage point of a new century, one finds some humorous items. For instance, "having a mortgage of over $10,000" was the twentieth item on the scale valued at 31 points; "having a mortgage of under $10,000" was thirty-seventh with only 17 points. The top ten life events and their values were:

1. Death of spouse—100
2. Divorce—73
3. Marital separation—65
4. Jail term—63
5. Death of close family member—63
6. Personal injury or illness—53
7. Marriage—50
8. Fired at work—47
9. Marital reconciliation—45
10. Retirement—45

One would think that a revised list for the 21st Century would probably include items such as "dangling chad ballots," terrorism attacks, anthrax, mailbox bombs, falling stock market, corporate fraud, *E.coli*, massive forest fires, flooding, draught, West Nile Virus, rampant unemployment, kidnapping/assaulting/murdering children, losing life savings, distrust of investing, distrust of FBI/CIA, snipers, and for specifically Catholic audiences, abusive clergy and silent bishops. However, the only revised list that I have seen does not include any of these items. It has been updated to include "major mortgage" (32 points) and "minor mortgage or loan" (17 points)

However, a new Scale for Children[1] (18 and Under) has been developed and includes many interesting life events such as "jail sentence of parent for over one year (75), discovery of being an adopted child (63), change in parent's financial status (45), and becoming a full fledged member of a church (31)."

Also, it is important to remember in this discussion that life events are only *one* source of stress, along with the general conditions of our lives and our belief system.

(For a continued discussion of the symptoms and effects of stress, please see Appendix C.)

Ways People Deal with Stress

During the course of writing this manual, I have interviewed many people, ranging in age from 12 to 82. It was interesting that when I asked them how they controlled their stress or what they did to lessen the degree of the symptoms common to stress, they first had to tell me in detail exactly where they found the most stress in their lives. (Experts tell us that one of the best means of controlling stress is to talk about it!)

The twelve-year-old revealed that most of her stress came from wanting to achieve expert status as a gymnast. A nineteen-year-old student at Ohio State University said that maintaining a high grade point level to keep him in the honors program caused him the most stress. Interestingly,

---

[1] For both of these revised scales, see Appendix A.

both of these young people said that they turned to games when they felt stressed out. The younger "went outside to play with her friends," while the other headed for a stint with Nintendo.

Most adults, after sharing what caused them stress, indicated that they prayed. It did not matter whether or not they were Christian, or whether or not they were churchgoers. They would ask, "Do you mean after prayer, what do I do to control stress?"

The *Serenity Prayer* was the most frequently mentioned prayer, which asks for the wisdom to know the difference between situations which they could control and situations where they had no control at all. The other prayers were divided between conversational prayer with God or rote prayers such as the *Our Father* or the *Rosary*.

The responses to "What do you do when you are really stressed out?" were (in descending frequency):
1. Pray
2. Talk to friends
3. Participate in intense physical activity (mostly running or walking)
4. Practice deep breathing exercises
5. Write in journals
6. Turn to yoga
7. Mentally compartmentalize worries and choose *not to worry* about particular situations
8. Practice guided imagery
9. Play games (Nintendo, bridge or other games on Internet)
10. Eat (or drink alcoholic beverages)

Controlling Reactions to Stress

While we often cannot control the things that are stressing us, we can control our reactions to those things. Experts tell us if we can change how we think, we can

change the way we feel. Here are five tips given in an Internet article:[2]
1. Make a list of the things that are causing your stress. Accept that you can't control everything on your list.
2. Take control of what you can.
3. Give yourself a break. Remember that you can't please everyone all the time. Also, it's okay to make mistakes every now and then.
4. Don't commit yourself to things you can't do or don't want to do.
5. Find someone to talk to (a person who is outside of the situation, if possible).

(For additional stress management techniques, please see Appendix C.)

From Stress to Crisis

While stress is disturbing and burdensome, crisis[3] is overwhelming distress, stress magnified a hundred times. A synonym for crisis is emergency, a time of great danger or trouble, with the potential of serious consequences following. Characteristics of crisis include a heightened state of emotional vulnerability (alarm, fear, anxiety, shock) that produces an acute need to regain a sense of psychological control and mind-body equilibrium. The profound tension of a crisis must be reduced so the person can return to some pre-crisis level of adaptation.

---

[2] "Stress: Who Has Time For It?" Information from Your Family Doctor, http://familydoctor.org/handouts/278.html

[3] The entire discussion on crisis here is adapted from two articles: "Crisis Intervention Techniques and Tips" by Mark Gorkin, MSW, LICSW, www. Businessknowhow.com/manage/crisis, 2001, and "Crisis Stress Reactions," no author listed, www.counseling. swt. edu/crisis Updated 1/3/02.

Crisis Reactions

People react differently, but the severity of the crisis usually has a direct effect on the severity of the reactions. For instance, a "mild" crisis might be defined as a work-related deadline or conflict with your boss. A severe crisis would be when you are fired.

Severe crises or severely stressful, sudden, or unusual events may overwhelm the usually effective coping skills that individuals have developed in order to deal with stressful situations. It is extremely important to realize that it is normal to experience some physical, mental and emotional reaction to such serious events—including depression. *(Please see Appendix D for a detailed list of reactions to severe crises.)*

Remember, these are normal reactions, but if any combinations of these symptoms persist, consult your personal physician or a mental health professional. Although painful, these normal reactions are part of the process of recovering from a loss or critical incident stress. While there is little anyone can do to take away these uncomfortable feelings, there are several things you can do to speed up the recovery process.

To Speed Up Recovery

1. Within the first 24 to 48 hours, periods of strenuous physical exercise alternated with relaxation will generally alleviate some of the physical reactions.
2. Structure your time, keep busy, and keep your life as normal as possible.
3. You're normal and having normal reactions – don't label yourself crazy.
4. Talk to people – talk is the most healing medicine.
5. Be aware of and avoid attempts to numb the pain with use of drugs or alcohol.
6. Reach out to others. Spend time with people you trust.

7. Help your peers by sharing feelings and checking out how they are doing.

The Trauma of September 11[4]

The terrorist attacks on September 11 are considered *traumatic* (as opposed to being described as stress or a crisis) and impacted many people. According to an American Psychological Association Fact Sheet,[5] people who were most seriously affected by the attacks fell into the three following categories:

1. Survivors of past traumatic events (e.g. refugees of wars, terrorism, or torture, and survivors of domestic violence, child abuse, or street crime). These individuals may have a heightened sense of vulnerability.
2. People who personally witnessed or were victims of the terrorist attack.
3. People who experienced traumatization from learning of relatives, friends and acquaintances who were subject to the violence or from *exposure to repeated media accounts of the trauma* (emphasis mine).

---

[4] The entire discussion here on Terrorism and Trauma is adapted from a variety of articles: "Coping with Terrorism," *American Psychological Association Fact Sheet*, www.APA HelpCenter: Psychology in Daily Life, undated, 2001; H.E. Marano, "Trauma: How to Cope After the Attacks," *Psychology Today*, www.psychologytoday.com/trauma, undated, 2001; McGrath, Ellen "Recovering from Trauma" and McGrath, Ellen, "Life Lessons," *Psychology Today*, www.psychology-today.com/trauma, undated, 2001; and "Significance of Post-Traumatic Stress," (no author given) http://aolsvc.health.webmd.aol.com/encyclopedia/article/2951.725. Undated, 2001.
[5] "Coping with Terrorism," op. cit.

Psychologist Hara Estroff Marano[6] states, "Anyone who saw the videotape of the second airplane hitting the south tower actually witnessed mass murder!" So, essentially anyone who watched television that day and saw the video re-runs of the attacks in New York or Washington experienced severe trauma, even though they were not present at the sites.

Marano goes on to say, "Those who lost loved ones endured further trauma. And rescue workers were exposed to scenes of devastation constantly. What magnifies the impact of this disaster for every American is the growing belief that it may not be a solitary event but one of a series of crises yet to be inflicted on us, that it is merely the opening salvo of a new kind of war."

In her article, "Recovering from Trauma," Dr. Ellen McGrath[7] states, "The human psyche has a tremendous capacity for recovery and even growth. Recovering from a traumatic experience requires that the painful emotions be thoroughly processed. Traumatic feelings can not be repressed or forgotten. If they are not dealt with directly, the distressing feelings and troubling events replay over and over in the course of a lifetime, creating a condition known as post-traumatic stress disorder."

The National Institute of Mental Health reports that "high levels of norepinephrine, a neurotransmitter released during stress, is one reason why people generally can remember emotionally arousing events better than other situations. Under the extreme stress of trauma, norepinephrine may act longer or more intensely, leading to the formation of abnormally strong memories that are then experienced as flashbacks or intrusions."[8] *(Please see a detailed list of reactions to acute trauma in Appendix E.)*

---

[6] H.E. Marano, "Trauma: How to Cope After the Attacks," op. cit.
[7] McGrath, Ellen op. cit.
[8] R Yehuda, "Psychoneuroendocrinology of Post Traumatic Stress Disorder." *Psychiatric Clinics of North America*, 1998; 21(2): 359-79.

Coping with Trauma

By definition, one's usual coping mechanisms do not prove sufficient after experiencing trauma or serious crisis. No matter how hard one tries, no matter how much a person wants to, one simply cannot cope well by using usual coping mechanisms. Usually, there has been no precedent for the crisis since most crises are unexpected and unwanted surprises, and thus, people have had no prior experience with dealing with issues of such severe nature. Further, terrorist acts are random, unprovoked, and intentional, and targeted at defenseless citizens.

In "When Disaster Strikes," Marano states three critically important factors known to diminish traumatic distress:

1. The most important factor is to **talk about the trauma**, to express the pain they feel. The struggle to put feelings and images of horror into words is therapeutic. Name the feelings. Feel the feelings.

2. Another crucial factor is **overcoming the sense of powerlessness or helplessness**, the sense that they have no control over their lives or over events. An important way that people did this after September 11 was by donating blood, donating money to the Red Cross and other charities, and offering to help a newly widowed mother of small children.

3. **Social support** is the third major factor in diminishing post-traumatic stress. People need to reach out to other people and be assured that the symptoms they are experiencing are normal—that there is no shame or stigma attached to their responses to trauma.

Four Stages of Recovery from Trauma

Dr. Ellen McGrath has made a significant contribution to the field of trauma management by identifying four distinct stages of recovery from profound traumatic stress.

1. **Stage One: Circuit-Breaking:** If overloaded, the human nervous system shuts down to just basics. People describe it as feeling numb, in shock, or "dead inside." Additionally, you lose from 50% to 90% of brain capacity, which is why you should never make a decision when you're in the trauma zone. Emotionally, you don't feel anything. Spiritually, you're disconnected. You have a spiritual crisis—or it doesn't mean anything at all.

2. **Stage Two: Return of Feelings:** Most people do not need professional help to work through their feelings which now return. They can do it through talking, and talking, and talking! They tell their story, over and over and over again—a hundred times. They identify, express, and describe their feelings, all of which is most beneficial. The more you feel, the more you heal!

3. **Stage Three: Constructive Action:** Making a difference even in the smallest, most seemingly insignificant way is extremely helpful: fly a flag, write a letter to the rescuers, or help someone else to become more grounded during the crisis. Stage Two and Stage Three go hand in hand: to go forward, you feel and you act. You must do both.

4. **Stage Four: Reintegration:** (The Good News!) It is possible to learn and grow at rates 100 times faster than at any other time because there is a door of opportunity. Growth can go at warp speed in

every domain of life. You can learn much that is deep and profound. Everyone who goes through this process ends up better, stronger, smarter, deeper, and more connected. Everyone who comes in contact with the formerly traumatized victims recognizes the change. Traumatic experiences are like broken bones of the soul. If you engage in the process of recovery, you get stronger. If you don't, the bones remain porous, with permanent holes inside, and you are considerably weaker.

The Blessing

We are dealing with one crisis after another these days, along with our own personal issues. Is crisis always a danger? Or is it sometimes an opportunity? The Chinese have a character in their alphabet which means danger. Another character means opportunity. When the Chinese join together the two characters for "danger" and "opportunity," it forms the character for "crisis." Our attitude about having to deal with a crisis can impact how well we respond to these crises. It is easy to see the danger in a crisis. Can we also find the opportunity hidden in the crisis? Perhaps the opportunity lies in driving us into the arms of God.

The Bible gives us many examples of times when God has brought good out of that which was not good. In the *Old Testament*, look at the life of Jacob's son, Joseph. In the *New Testament*, look at Jesus' suffering and death. Because of the severity of trauma, people move beyond habitual ways of responding to stress. For example, a person may allow himself for the first time to become more dependent on others, to reach out for resources, and/or experiment with new or improved methods of problem solving.

Father J. Bryan Hehir, president and CEO of Catholic Charities, noted, "*The Washington Post*, not noticeably a religious journal, made the comment about two months after September 11, that when the television commentators wanted to know what the mind of the country was like after the disaster, they asked psychologists. But without any detriment to psychologists, the *Post* made notice of the fact that where people went to deal with the sense of radical vulnerability was to churches, synagogues and mosques. So we gathered and prayed, and we gathered and reflected, and we gathered and reached for a source of support that was larger than we were. Because the crisis was larger than we were."[9]

What are some of the other blessings resulting from these major crises? To name a few:

Concerning the terrorist attacks:
1. a renewed sense of patriotism
2. a greater awareness of the beauty of life
3. an intentional desire to spend more time with family and loved ones
4. a trend to coziness in home decor, comfort foods

Concerning the Church sexual abuse crisis:
1. a greater awareness of protecting our children
2. a sense of compassion for abusive clergy and their victims
3. a greater appreciation of the many, many healthy and holy priests who serve us
4. the realization that more lay involvement is necessary for future prevention
5. realizing our own call to personal holiness

Concerning the economic crisis:
1. return to a simpler, less consumer-oriented lifestyle

---

[9] "Leadership and Hope in a Time of Crisis and Conflict," speech to the Annual Catholic Charities USA Conference, Chicago, August 2, 2002.

2. an enormous sense of gratitude for the material goods and wealth which have not been diminished by the crumbling economy
3. a new awareness of the enormous inequity between the first and third worlds
4. becoming more cautious in expenditures
5. re-evaluating our priorities
6. a greater sensitivity to the poor, the homeless
7. ethics classes now required for many MBAs

And the Curse

On the other hand, not all people take advantage of the potential opportunities in crisis. For instance, if a person lacks support or is ashamed of showing emotion or neediness, an individual in crisis or trauma may regressively withdraw or turn to escapist behavior and other dysfunctional adaptations.

McGrath writes, "People's worst defenses emerge in response to overwhelming stress. Over time, a pattern of destructive behavior becomes clear. Experience has shown that for the first year after a disaster, rates of spousal abuse increase dramatically. Divorce rates rise 50%. Substance abuse rises 60% to 70%. Depression rates soar. A week after the September 11 attack, more than 70% of Americans acknowledged experiencing depression, even though it was not socially acceptable to do so."[10]

Also, while most crises were normally thought to be time-limited, that may not be the case with the September 11 attacks. Usually, within one to six weeks, a person would regain a state of equilibrium. However, with the possibility of more terrorist strikes, anthrax deaths, possible war with Iraq, or other unforeseeable events in the future, many people will vacillate in their recovery. With this type of prolonged stress with one crisis after another, one soon

---

[10] McGrath, "Recovering from Trauma," op. cit.

feels as if he or she is permanently riding on a roller coaster of emotions.

Also, it was previously thought that there was a learning curve for coping with crises and that effective coping with an initial crisis often helped prepare an individual for a positive response and better management of subsequent crises or trauma effects. The theory was that men who faced combat in Vietnam or Desert Storm may have experienced several of the same feelings of combat during the terrorist attacks and were better able to cope with them than the person who did not have similar experiences. However, that theory is now being questioned. McGrath writes, "Traumas activate all unfinished business and stir up all trauma that has occurred to us before. Those previously exposed will be more debilitated in the current crisis than those who haven't been exposed. They're dealing not just with the current crisis but with horrendous experiences from the past."

She continues, "People vary tremendously in their capacity to handle traumatic stress and to work it through. They also vary in the time and pacing of recovery and the strategies they employ. Everyone does the best he or she is able to do. One of the worst actions individuals can take is to judge others. Judging disconnects people from each other. It is also inappropriate because no one has the full range of information on which to base judgments. Don't judge."[11]

(Please see Appendix E for a list of additional "Trauma Do's and Don'ts.")

---

[11] McGrath, op. cit.

FOOD FOR THOUGHT

"All shall be well, and all shall be well, and all manner of thing shall be well."
Julian of Norwich

"There is nothing permanent except change."
Heraclitus

Prayerful Suggestions

1. Read Psalm 4:

I
When I call, answer me, O my just God,
    you who relieve me when I am in distress:
    Have pity on me, and hear my prayer!

II
Men of rank, how long will you be dull of heart?
    Why do you love what is vain and seek after
    falsehood?
Know that the LORD does wonders for his faithful
    one;
    the LORD will hear me when I call upon him.
Tremble, and sin not;
    reflect, upon your beds, in silence.
Offer just sacrifices,
    and trust in the LORD.

III
Many say, "Oh, that we might see better times!"
O LORD, let the light of your countenance shine
    upon us!
You put gladness into my heart,
    more than when grain and wine abound.
As soon as I lie down, I fall peacefully asleep,
    for you alone, O LORD, bring security to my
    dwelling.

2. Place all of your worries and cares in the Lord's hands in prayer.

3. Offer your next Mass for the people/situations which are causing you distress.

Psychological Suggestions

More Helpful Hints for
Post-Traumatic Coping[12]

1) ***Strive for Realistic Control:*** Do not try to achieve an absolute sense of control of your external environment, as this will invariably leave one feeling more at risk. The *Serenity Prayer* is relevant and appropriate here:

Grant me the serenity to accept the things I cannot change, the courage to change the things I can, and the wisdom to know the difference.

2. ***Seek Sources of Support:*** Find sources of support when feeling the need for nurturance or reassurance. Are there supportive/nurturing resources available at home, at work, through the church, with friends – in person, over the phone, on the Internet? Is there an on-line or off-line support group available?

3. ***Take Some Concrete Action Steps:*** Focus on two or three action steps that would help you feel a small but significant degree of enhanced safety and security.

---

[12] "Crisis Intervention Techniques and Tips" by Mark Gorkin, MSW, LICSW, www. Businessknowhow.com/manage/crisis, undated, 2001.

4. *Explore the Need for Counseling:* Counseling is an option. If in the next few weeks the post-traumatic symptoms are not subsiding, professional guidance is indicated. Also, if you are feeling that you need to vent your feelings in ways that might either hurt yourself or someone else, please seek professional help immediately!

5. *Communicate Optimism:* Reaffirm that post-traumatic stress is natural, that crisis can heighten a person's problem solving capacity, enhance a person's communal circle of support, and that the grief process may be a catalyst for potent healing and growth producing energy.

For Reflection and Discussion:[13]

1. Where were you on September 11, 2001? What were your reactions then?

_____
_____
_____
_____
_____

2. List the current stressful events or situations in your life which you have experienced since September 11:
   1. _____
   2. _____
   3. _____
   4. _____

3. Have you experienced any of the symptoms common to stress (Appendix C), crisis (Appendix D), or trauma (Appendix E)? Describe.

_____
_____

---

[13] Please see **Group Guidelines for Discussions,** page 143.

4. Can you remember a time in your life when you had similar feelings or symptoms? What happened then? How did you cope?

5. Describe the blessings that you have experienced as the result of crisis.

CHAPTER TWO

NAMING OUR FEARS/ OWNING OUR LOSSES

"Let me assert my firm belief that the only thing we have to fear is fear itself—nameless, unreasoning terror."
Franklin D. Roosevelt

Opening Prayer

God our Father, you are so good. But much of what is happening in our world is not good. Scripture gives us a sure knowledge of your goodness and reassures us that you can bring good out of that which is not good.

Pour out your Spirit upon us as we cope with the communal crises in our world and with the personal crises in our own lives. Help us hear and receive the Gospel message of reconciliation and healing with ready and responsive hearts. Strengthen our desire to be your faithful people. And give us your peace and new life during this time. We ask this in Jesus' name. Amen.

Where Were You on September 11?

Many people will remember forever where they were on September 11, 2001, just as older folks can remember exactly where they were on December 7, 1941, when Pearl Harbor was attacked or on November 22, 1963, when John F. Kennedy was assassinated.

I first heard about the terrorist attacks when I was playing golf with our Tuesday Morning Women's League. My husband, who is the controller of the country club, drove up in a golf cart with this unbelievable news. It was unfathomable at first. I simply could not understand what he was saying. Surely he didn't mean the Twin Towers in New York or the Pentagon in Washington. He must be mistaken.

To her credit, one of my partners understood exactly what he was saying and, urging us to hold hands right there on the 12th green, she led us in prayer for the victims and for our country. It is a moment I will never forget.

We immediately left the golf course and returned to the clubhouse where I watched television only for a few moments. I just could not take the intensity of what was being said and shown. I became very, very cold and drove the short distance to my home.

That afternoon, as I continued watching television accounts of the tragedy, I became so cold that I had to take a hot shower, put on flannel pajamas (the warmest thing I own, living in South Florida!) and cover myself with a blanket. And I still was shivering for hours afterward into the early evening. My doctor said it was a classic case of shock.

The Grieving Process

What was your first reaction to hearing or seeing on television the actual events of the terrorist attacks on the World Trade Center and the Pentagon? If you were like most people, you were numb with disbelief. "Oh my God, this can't be happening!" "This isn't real!" "This is surreal!" "Tell me this is fiction!" All of these statements, along with the feelings of being numb with disbelief, are classic examples of **shock and denial.** "This can't be happening to us!" "This can't be happening here!"

The next feelings and comments you experienced may have been something along the lines of, "Where are they going to attack next?" "Are we safe here?" "Is our city safe?" "Where can we flee?" "What are we going to do now?" "What will the President say?" "Where is the President? Is he safe?" All of these statements are appropriate to the experience of **fear and panic.**

Next comes a sense of **rage and helplessness.** "How dare they!" or "Oh, no, how could these people possibly do this to us?" "I (we) can't do anything about this. Thousands of people were killed and there is nothing we can do to un-do it!"

Eventually, rage and helplessness are transformed into **guilt and ambivalence.** "How can I feel like I'm 'getting back to normal' so soon after such a horrible event?" "Why did I (we) survive when all of those innocent people were killed?" "Maybe we deserved it." "Americans really are arrogant—superficial—greedy."

Focused anger is the beginning of the healing process. We say, "Damn it! I don't like this situation. But how do I (we) make the best of it?"

Exploration of options leads to a **new identity**. "Yes, the Homeland Security Program is just what we need!" "Yes, let's support the militia in every airport security system." You are no longer a victim.

Acceptance of the situation as in "the glass is half-empty and half-full." That is, we choose to see not only the destructiveness of the event but we see the opportunity to strengthen our pride in our country, to honor and assist the survivors of Ground Zero, to transform pain into power as much as possible.

These seven phases—
1) shock and denial;
2) fear and panic;

3) rage and helplessness;
4) guilt and ambivalence;
5) focused anger;
6) exploration and new identity; and
7) acceptance

are the seven stages of the grief process identified and described by Mark Gorkin, MSW, LICSW, and published on the Internet in an article entitled "Traumatic Stress/Crisis Intervention Techniques and Tips," (Website cited above, July, 2002.)

It is interesting to note how they are both similar to and different from the classic five stages of grieving described by Dr. Kubler-Ross:
1) Denial
2) Anger
3) Bargaining
4) Depression
5) Acceptance

There is a sequential order to both of these descriptions of the grieving process. But a person may pass over one stage or make two steps forward and, then, inexplicably fall back to a previous emotional state or stage.

The Healing Process

Think about your own personal experience during personal crises. During public crises? What were your reactions, responses? Surprise? Shock? Anger? Confusion?

As we read in the last chapter, one of the characteristics of crisis and trauma includes a heightened state of emotional vulnerability (alarm, fear, anxiety, shock).

"What did it mean, September 11, 2001?" asked Fr. Bryan Hehir in his speech to Catholic Charities USA. "One begins with simply shock and massive devastation. There is no other way than to begin with the facts—the facts of human destruction and psychological shock, personal, familial, national. The shock and the devastation created a sense of radical vulnerability in the most powerful nation the world has ever known in recorded history."[14]

Jesus tells us over one hundred times in Scripture: "Fear not. Be not afraid." But, if we are honest with ourselves, many of us *are* afraid! Many of us *are* hurting. Many of us *are* angry! Many of us *are* worried about our present and future security. Many of us are so very, very *scared*.

This reminds me of one of my favorite stories which concerns the family of a Protestant minister. One night there was a terrible storm. The thunder was crashing and the lightning was flashing. His little five-year-old son cried out from his room, "Daddy, Daddy, come and take care of me. I am so scared!"

The father cried back, "Don't be afraid! You know that God loves you and that God will take care of you!"

"Yes, Daddy, I know," the son yelled back. "I know that God loves me and God will take care of me, but right now I need a 'God with skin on'!"

Like the little boy, we would all love to have a "God with skin on!" We would love to be able to believe that no harm ever will befall us. We want to believe that God will protect us, as the psalmist reassures us in Psalm 91: "God will put his angels over us." Psalm 23 assures us that the Lord will always be our shepherd.

In Scripture we hear that God loves us so much that he will take better care of us than the sparrows or the lilies in the field. In spite of God's promises, we focus on the reality of events—tragedies do happen. We wonder where God is when things go wrong. We wonder how God could let such things happen.

Nevertheless, when these unexplainable tragedies occur, we must trust more than ever in the mystery of God

---

[14] Hehir, op. cit.

and know that God walks with us, on the mountaintop and in the valley of the shadow of death.

The Suffering of Job

Sometimes, we also feel like Job. We're tired of the suffering. We can't take the pain or the disappointment or the frustration much longer. Everything seems to be going wrong. Sometimes we cannot even name our pain—is it anger or frustration or depression or loss or "all of the above?" We want to be able to carry on. We want to remember who we are and *whose* we are and *believe,* but, it is quite difficult sometimes, especially in the midst of tragedy.

One day when I was dealing with a number of serious problems, I became quite overwhelmed. In addition to everything else going on in our lives, both my husband and I were scheduled for biopsies the next day. The biopsies and all the other problems turned out fine. But I still remember the cynicism I felt that day. Thinking of Job, I looked up to Heaven and sarcastically asked, "What next? Boils?" And I thought of St. Teresa's famous line, "If this is the way you treat your friends, no wonder you have so few." And people do blame God!

We Blame God

Once in a funeral home many years ago, I stood next to a very dear friend whose teenaged son had committed suicide. As her friends and neighbors came forward to comfort her, so many of them said things like, "God just wanted another angel, so he took your son home." Or "This is God's will. You just have to accept it."

I wanted to scream out with all my heart and soul, "No! This is not God's will! Jesus came to bring us life —not death at the age of sixteen! Our God is a loving and compassionate God. He does not want my friend and her husband to suffer like this!"

That was the first time, I guess, that I really, really questioned "Why do bad things happen to good people?" I struggled with that question for a long time until a priest friend of mine helped me with his explanation. He said that so often, people tend to blame God for these horrible events. "In fact, Sue," he said, "I don't think God has anything at all to do with these tragedies." He then explained that most tragedies happen for one of three reasons:

> 1. Decisions which we ourselves make. For instance, if we choose to smoke cigarettes and forty years later, we are diagnosed with lung cancer, don't blame it on God. This is a consequence of a decision that we made.
>
> 2. Decisions which other people make, over which we have no control. If a person decides to drive after drinking, there may be certain terrible consequences.
>
> 3. The results of natural processes. For instance, the aging process, genetic diseases, natural disasters.

And, of course, there is a fourth category called "Mystery." When none of the other three reasons apply, we must simply accept the fact that sometimes we can find no logic, no rhyme or reason, no rational explanation. Just mystery. This is when we must "let God be God."

Universal Suffering

After crisscrossing the United States and Canada during many years of presenting Isaiah Missions, I have learned that one factor remained constant—universal suffering. No matter where I went, no matter the wealth or the poverty of the community, the education or lack of it, people were suffering.

Why do people suffer? Same three reasons as above. Mainly, the first two where either people make decisions themselves or other people make decisions which directly affect the people.

I will never forget the Mexican-American mother whom I met in southwest Texas several years ago at an Isaiah parish mission. She had three young daughters, ranging in age from nine to about thirteen. She came to me one night after a session with tears in her eyes and fear in her heart. "My husband, he abuses my daughters," she stammered in slightly broken English. "He has sex with them. I can tell no one. He won't stop. He says he will kill me if I tell anyone."

I asked if she had gone to her pastor for any advice or comfort. "No," she said, looking over her shoulder even though we had privacy as she spoke. "But, I know—no divorce allowed! My neighbor told me so. And no police! They will put my husband in jail, and then we have no food, no house."

In this woman's mind, there was absolutely no solution to this horrible problem which she was facing, knowing that her daughters were being abused and feeling that she was unable to protect them. I asked her permission to discuss this situation with the pastor of the parish where we were giving this mission. She hesitantly said, "Yes, but no jail!" And I told her, I could not promise that but if that did happen, the pastor would find ways to help her and her children survive. I *promised* her—and then held my breath as I spoke to the pastor later that night.

Exactly as I had hoped, the pastor was able to help her for there was an extensive social system existing for women in her situation who felt that they had no way out! Several weeks later, the husband was in jail, and the mother and daughters were in a safe house where the mother was getting job training and the whole family was safe and secure.

I have found that cultural, systemic or endemic suffering in this world, such as the three tragedies we have been focusing on (terrorism, sexual abuse, and corporate fraud) are caused by decisions based on an abuse of power. In all three cases, this abuse of power resulted in destruction, deprivation, greed, and fear. In Maria's case, the abuse of power certainly was evident in the highly dysfunctional family.

Abandonment

We are *radically vulnerable*, now more than ever! But, still, we must name, accept, and own our feelings, whatever they are. If we are being honest about our feelings, sometimes we may feel like the psalmist who cries out in Psalm 22: *"My God, my God, why have you abandoned me?"*

When we feel abandoned by everyone including God, we want to cry out, *"Father, take this cup away from me. I don't want to drink it any more. Why have you abandoned me? Come back, be at my side, rescue me."*

We know that when Jesus felt abandoned, he acceded, saying, *"Your will, not mine, be done."* And we know that God did not abandon Jesus. However, it is precisely because Jesus *did* drink the bitter cup and because he was not rescued that salvation is ours. Jesus, human in all things including pain and suffering, died on the cross, was buried and rose again on the third day. It is because Jesus Christ shed his blood for us that we have been saved, that no matter what we have done, no matter what has been done to us, or what will happen to us in the future, we are God's chosen ones.

We must remember that no matter how we feel, no matter what the world may tell us, we have been purchased for God, *"not with perishable things like silver or gold but with the precious blood of Christ as of a spotless unblemished lamb."*

Suffering: Both Hope and Challenge

In 1995, the U.S. Bishops included a reflection on suffering in their document concerning the laity.[15] "Often people can go the extra mile for others because they have been spiritually formed through suffering. For Christians, suffering is both hope and challenge."

The bishops continued, "St. Paul writes: *'We know that affliction makes for endurance, and endurance for tested virtue, and tested virtue for hope'* (Rom. 5:3-4). The laity of our Church are moved to act on behalf of those in need because they have come to know Christ in the depths of their own suffering. Some have been betrayed by their marriage partners. Others, many of whom are women, have endured physical and emotional abuse. Children have had to adjust to divorce and separated parents. And parents have known helplessness as their children leave the Church, become addicted to drugs, or accept an ethic of casual sex.

"Others," the bishops continue, "have experienced prejudice or discrimination because of their language or racial background. As people have lost their jobs, their homes, or their loved ones, they have also found the abundance of God's mercy; they know the hope of which St. Paul speaks. In the darkness that surrounds them they discover the light of Christ and the truth that 'The way of perfection passes by way of the Cross' (*Catechism of the Catholic Church*, No. 2015). They are ready to help others along the way and in so doing become signs of hope."

An interesting and prophetic passage of this 1995 document also suggests, "As we enter the third millennium,

---

[15]"Called and Gifted for the Third Millennium," U. S. Catholic Bishops, Publication No. 54002, USCC, Washington, DC, 1995, p 5.

we may well see more collective suffering. . . . New strains of disease, persistent economic instability, large movements of displaced persons, and a multiplicity of wars are already a reality and may increase." Little did the bishops know then of September 11 and the other crises we all would face only six years hence.

Name the Pain!

Does God ever get angry? Does Jesus get angry? Of course. Just read many passages in the Old Testament to see the "wrath of God" in full view. And Jesus certainly was angry when he threw the money-changers out of the temple. Is God ever sad? We know the answer to that one, too. Jesus wept over Jerusalem. Jesus knows what it is to suffer, too. He was betrayed, denied, abandoned. He was killed by the very people he came to save. One-sixth of Jesus' apostles (Judas and Peter) hurt him badly, and the others, except for John, abandoned him in his moment of trial.

It's appropriate and normal not just to have feelings, but to have *strong* feelings in response to crises. We see Jesus experiencing justifiable anger in Scriptures when he furiously drives the moneychangers from the temple. We see him weeping profoundly over Jerusalem, *"Like a mother hen, how I yearn to take you under my wing."*

Sacred Rage

Rev. Kevin Culligan, O.Carm., wrote of his outrage when he realized what was happening in the Church during the height of the abuse crisis. His article is entitled, "Sacred Rage and Rebuilding the Church."[16]

---

[16] Kevin Culligan, a priest and licensed psychologist, is a Discalced Carmelite friar currently serving as the coordinator for ministry planning for the order's Immaculate Heart of Mary Province. *National Catholic Reporter,* September 13, 2002.

Describing the scene in the Temple, he wrote, "When Jesus discovered that the religious leaders had allowed the moneychangers and animal merchants to make a market place of the temple area, he became violent. Jesus quickly made a crude whip from flax and lashed out at the offenders. He drove them and the animals from the temple area. He overturned the moneychangers' tables, scattering coins across the floor."

He concludes his article writing, "Unfortunately, many current spiritualities regard strong emotion—fear, joy, anger, sadness, hope, pity—as obstacles to spiritual growth. Jesus exemplifies the opposite. His emotions moved him to fulfill his vocation as Yahweh's faithful servant to an abandoned and neglected people—teaching, preaching, healing, exorcising, building community, celebrating life, and even purifying the temple. Our emotions, too—our rage as well as our compassion—are sacred. They are God's gifts that enable us, the risen body of Jesus, to continue his work on earth, especially rebuilding his church."

No More Denial

In order to allow the healing process to begin, it is so important to admit, to acknowledge, and to name the pain, whether it is severe, serious, or mild in degree. We must look honestly at how and where we have been hurt. Many choose to deny any pain, which is a typical American *macho* thing to do. Many are unable or unwilling to admit pain since they view it as a sign of weakness.

All of us (especially men) need encouragement to know that it is perfectly legitimate and acceptable to say, "Yes, we *are* worried about future terrorist attacks; we *are* angry with the bishops these days; we *are* scared now that we have lost our life savings." It is not a sign of weakness or paranoia but a healthy admission of reality. It is the beginning of healing.

Consider just these three major events—September 11, the crisis in the Church, and a fallen stock market. There are any number of feelings that people may have in response, for example: ***Anger, Rage, Frustration, Sadness, Grief, Distrust, Fear, Anxiety, Fury, Confusion, Apprehension, Disgust, Insecurity, Betrayal, Abandonment, Doubt, Shame, and Embarrassment.***

Feelings may fluctuate quickly from one to another, or we may have any combination of feelings, all at the same time. All of these feelings are normal reactions to crisis and trauma.

Name Our Losses

Just as we must name our feelings, we must name our losses. What have we lost collectively? What have we lost individually? Consider the hierarchical triangle of psychologist Abraham Maslow which puts physical needs at the basic, bottom level of needs, followed by safety and security as the second. His theory states that unless these basic needs are met in a person's life, the other needs (for love, for belonging, and for self-actualization) cannot even be addressed, let alone be met. With the terrorist attacks, our sense of safety and security is imperiled. With losing all or part of our life savings or our retirement funds, our need to provide food, clothing, and shelter may suddenly take priority over all other needs. We have lost: ***Trust, Security, Safety, World Peace, Happiness, Pride, Life Savings, Sleep, Health, and Peace of Mind.*** I'm sure you will be able to add other losses to this list.

Just as we need to acknowledge our feelings and our losses, we need to acknowledge our confusion and ambivalence in the world today. Sometimes faith in *what should be* does not match the reality of events in the world. At the same time, we must give other people permission to identify and name their pain, wounds, losses. We may not dismiss or diminish *any* of the negative feelings which people may be feeling. One of the worst things you could say is, "Oh, you shouldn't feel that way!"

Mourning – Not an Option

There is a brighter side to all of this, but for right now, it is important to name our woundedness and our losses. There will be a time for healing. But, first we must mourn what was lost. Mourning is not *an option but* a *necessity.* Mourning is not a pleasant feeling, but it is a feeling we must accept if we are to be healed. There is no other way with the grief process—we can't go under it or over it or around it—we must go *through* it in order for healing to occur.

At the height of the church crisis, my parish priests were saying very little about the scandal at Mass, and it was "church as usual." As more and more bad news came out that, for the most part, these priests did not address, the angrier I became. Not at the abusive priests—but at the bishops whom I felt should be held accountable. As time went by, I grew increasingly angry with my own parish priests because they appeared to be dismissing or, at best, minimalizing this crisis.

And then Archbishop Rembert Weakland of Milwaukee, one of my theological and pastoral heroes, was accused of a decades-old incident and resigned in shame. The article in the secular newspaper pointed out what a wonderful man he was, what valuable service he had provided as one of the principle writers of the bishops' documents on peace and justice and on the economy. I felt as if I were reading an obituary of a very dear friend!

The following morning at Mass, when not a word was mentioned about Archbishop Weakland or any of the other current problems, I realized I felt like *a great big huge funeral was going on but that I was the only person mourning.*

Another Funeral

Eventually, as my anger generalized, I began to be angry with *everyone*–my husband, my kids, my grandchildren, myself, even the postman. I soon realized that I needed professional counseling in order to sort this all out. I explained my great sense of frustration, anger, powerlessness, and confusion to a very caring and compassionate counselor. Together we explored the situation, my intense feelings, possible explanations and possible solutions.

This wise woman asked me, after several sessions, if I could remember another time in my life when I had felt so shocked, so angry, so frustrated, so powerless, so confused. Amazingly, I was able to immediately identify a situation which met all of those criteria. I hadn't thought about it in ages. As I described it to my counselor, her mouth fell wide open in surprise.

The incident that I am speaking of happened when my mother died in 1990, more than ten years ago. I had been giving a parish workshop in the Houma, Louisiana diocese when my brother called in the middle of the night to tell me that my mother had died. The gracious people I was staying with were just wonderful and helped me to arrange a flight for the first thing in the morning to Tucson where my parents had retired. Their friends drove me to the New Orleans airport, several hours away, where I purchased my ticket and checked my luggage.

With about two hours to wait since the plane had been delayed, I sent them home. There was no need for them, a working couple, to wait with me. At that point, I decided to call my father in Tucson.

I told him that I was calling to let him know what flight I would be on and what time I would be getting there.

I will never forget his response. "Why are you coming, Susan?"

"Why am I coming? What a ridiculous question to ask me," I thought to myself. "I'm coming to help you

make all of the arrangements for the funeral and everything," I responded.

"Well, you don't need to come. Mom has already been cremated. There's not going to be any funeral."

I was so shocked that I didn't know what to say. I just couldn't imagine that my mother wouldn't have a funeral and some sort of a service. Neither of my parents are Catholic, so I knew not to expect a Mass. But no funeral? No service? Nothing?

I hung up and stood there in a phone booth in the middle of the New Orleans airport in shock! *"I can't believe this,"* I thought. *"This can't be happening!"* But it was happening and reality set in as I realized that there was no way I could go back to the Houma parish. (How does one explain that there is no funeral for her own mother?) It didn't make any sense to go home to Florida either, since I was scheduled to give a mission the following week in another parish in Houma. I had no place to go. And I was alone. I felt abandoned by my father. My brothers would not be going to Tucson either. I had no chance to say "Goodbye" to my mother or share the loss with my family. This was surreal! *I felt like a great big funeral should be going on . . . but I was the only one mourning!*

After my counselor closed her gaping mouth, she asked with great concern, "What did you do then?"

"Well," I told her, "after deciding to take a cab into New Orleans and getting a hotel room, I felt such a great need for prayer that I visited the magnificent St. Louis Cathedral in the heart of the city."

When I slipped into one of the pews and began praying, I realized that I was offering my own funeral Mass for my mother. I knew the words of the liturgy by heart and I went through the whole service, silently proclaiming the Rite of Introduction, the "Lord have mercy, Christ, have mercy," the "Gloria" and so on. (And, of course, I could now joke with my counselor, "With all of my experience of preaching parish missions, I gave an excellent homily, too.")

Returning to the memory, I recalled that I had to imagine the consecration and receiving Holy Communion. But, since I have a very vivid imagination, this was not a difficult task. I said my prayers of thanksgiving for my mother's life, with tears streaming down my face.

At just that moment, a group of people came up the aisle behind me with their tour guide, who was saying something like, "And on our left is the beautiful rose window." I could just imagine him pointing to me, saying, "And on your right is our resident mourner!" This thought struck me as very comical, and my tears turned into quiet, gentle, inner laughter. With the Mass over, I was able to walk, smiling, out into the sunshine of a glorious day! My mother had been honorably buried, and she was smiling, too.

The week after I shared all of this with my counselor, I went through an imaginary "ritual funeral" for the Church as I knew and loved it before this crisis. I found peace and comfort again. My perception of the *institution*al church had changed, but my faith in God was not diminished in the least.

However, since we are being honest here, I must admit that over time I continue to find additional levels of distrust with this issue. Just because I had this ritual funeral, or just because the bishops have agreed to a certain policy does not make the Church scandal go away for me. On the other hand, lay groups like *Voice of the Faithful* which is now 25,000-strong give me hope.

"Building the Kingdom"

"Christ alone is the cornerstone on which it is possible to solidly build one's existence. A new generation of builders is needed. Moved not by fear or violence, but by the urgency of genuine love, they must learn to build, brick by brick, the City of God."

Echoing Pope John Paul II's comments, I believe that a new generation of builders is needed to build the kingdom in our world today, a world based on love rather than terror. We need to rebuild the Church, the Body of Christ, in a world of trust. We need to restore the business community in a world of sound ethics and morality.

And, first we need to name our pain and own our losses. Let the healing process begin!

Closing Prayer

Loving God, We know that your love for us is beyond understanding and that when we weep, you weep. Help us to know that you are with us, walking at our side. We offer our feelings to you, asking for reconciliation, strength, and healing.

Comfort us as we taste the bitter wine of anger and betrayal and the salty tears of fear and doubt. Help us to acknowledge and ease the suffering and pain of your broken and suffering Body. We ask this in your most holy name. Amen.

Food for Thought
"We must not fear fear."
St. Francis de Sales

Psalm 121
I lift up my eyes toward the mountains;
    whence shall help come to me?
My help is from the LORD,
    who made heaven and earth.

May he not suffer your foot to slip;
    May he slumber not who guards you:

> Indeed he neither slumbers nor sleeps,
> > the guardian of Israel.
> The LORD is your guardian; the LORD is your
> > shade;
> > he is beside you at your right hand.
> The sun shall not harm you by day, nor the
> > moon by night.
> The LORD will guard your coming and your going, both now and forever.

Psychological Suggestions Concerning Any Private or Public Crisis in Your Life[17]:

"10 Healing Steps for Coping with Crisis, Trauma, And Other Things That Go Bump in the Night"

The list below has been adapted from an article by Carol Razza, Ph.D., a clinical psychologist appointed to the Diocese of Palm Beach "Blue Ribbon Committee." She also served as the facilitator of the listening sessions held throughout the diocese during the recent clergy crisis. Her article originally was entitled "10 Healing Ways to Cope with the Clergy Crisis," but has been adapted and broadened to apply to other crises. The original article was one of the motivators for the development of the new "Building the Kingdom in a Changing World" parish mission.

1. Speak the truth in love. Own your feelings. Your feelings are not right or wrong; they just are. Don't judge others who may not feel as you do. Healing begins when we speak out about our hurts to someone who will listen and understand our pain.

---

[17] Adapted from "Ways to Cope with the Church Crisis" by Carol Razza, Ph.D. a clinical psychologist who was invited to facilitate the Listening Sessions in the Diocese of Palm Beach.

2. Confront your emotional pain—your shock, fear, anger and grief. Recognize that the hurt that has occurred may have been very unfair and that these steps are not meant to minimize the hurt involved. However, see these situations as an opportunity for healing and for growth. Realize that these feelings are normal after a crisis or traumatic experience. Do not try to avoid them or minimize them. Face them; deal with them.

3. Realize that you are the only person responsible for your own feelings and for healing the wounds within you.

4. Start releasing anger, sadness, grief, fear, and worries in healthy ways such as talking, drawing, writing, physical activity, and socializing.

5. Realize that forgiveness and healing can only be appropriate after you have processed your fear, anger, and grief. However, also realize that you can set goals now for healing and forgiveness. Recognize that to continue to dwell on the anger or fear will literally destroy your physical health and cause you great mental suffering.

6. Speak to the right people. Negative talk, blame, or gossip only feeds the hurt. It is important to speak to those individuals that can foster healing, not further pain. Do not hesitate to seek professional counseling.

7. Do not over-generalize. Absolute statements such as "the whole Church is. . . ."or "all Arab-Americans are. . . ." are distortions and will feed your anger. Stay focused on the facts, not the media's presentation of the facts.

8. Frequent the sacraments. We are blessed to have the sacraments to strengthen us. Recognize that in your midst, at every celebration of the Holy Mass, is the body, blood,

soul and divinity of our Lord. Nothing can be more important. We all need to be aware of the condition of our heart. God will heal our church and our world as we all humble ourselves and seek God's presence. Be open to forgiveness.

9. Overcoming the sense of helplessness is crucial. One important way is reaching out to and helping others, even if only in very small ways or random acts of kindness.

10. Be change makers. Focus on solutions, not continually on the problems. Get involved in making positive changes.

Practical Suggestions

1. Write down your most intense feelings every day for a week. Write a sentence or two about the intensity of your feeling.
2. Speak to someone you trust about these feelings. (Priests, pastoral staff, professional counselors).
3. Give yourself permission to vent your feelings in healthy ways such as prayer, writing, talking, exercise, meditation.

Prayerful Suggestions

1. Write a letter to God, thanking God for all of the good things that are happening in your life right now; for all of the happiness and joy you are experiencing in various aspects of your life. List your blessings of family, friends, children, grandchildren, marriage, vocation, faith, etc.

2. Read Psalm 121 and memorize the last line: "The LORD will guard my coming and going, both now and forever." Repeat this whenever you are feeling fearful or anxious.

For Reflection and Small Group Discussion:

1. Remember a time when you were genuinely afraid. Describe your feelings, reactions, and responses. How was your fear resolved?

2. Describe a situation that is causing distress in your life right now, or a situation which has caused distress in the past. (Do not analyze it, blame anyone for it, or try to fix it.)

3. Name some of your feelings about this situation and rank them from 1(very intense) to 10 (very slight).

4. What are some healthy ways of venting these feelings?

5. Name some blessings which have already come from the three major crises: terrorism, the church scandal, and the economic decline.

CHAPTER THREE

UNFORGIVENESS—A MAJOR STUMBLING BLOCK

"Nothing causes us to so nearly resemble God as the forgiveness of injuries."
— St. John of Chrysostom

Opening Prayer

Gracious God, we ask you to transform our pain, our losses, and our confusion into wisdom and acceptance. We ask you to help us overcome any stumbling blocks that obstruct or prolong the rebuilding process. We ask you to help us to deal with our unforgiveness of others and to accept our own forgiveness. We ask this through Jesus, who in his life showed mercy and forgiveness to all. Amen.

Stumbling Blocks

What are some of the stumbling blocks we might face in coping with everyday stress and the dramatic events of our times? What may be prohibiting or prolonging the process of reconciliation and healing? Denial? Anger? Excessive Fear? Anxiety? ("Protect us from *unnecessary* anxiety.") Unforgiveness? Powerlessness? The sense that our faith is not strong enough?

We do not tend to think of these responses to trauma or crisis as "good" feelings because they are painful. However, good can come out of them by alerting us to the need for change. In a similar way in our bodies, fever or pain alerts us that something is wrong, something needs to be changed to eliminate the cause of the pain. In this way, some of these stumbling blocks can be helpful, perhaps even necessary to the healing process.

Denial may be the only way that some people can cope with trauma. Excessive anger or unnecessary anxiety may be appropriate, also, during transition to better coping skills. The sense that our faith is not strong enough may prod us to strengthen our faith, to seek God in the present moment, to beg God to come to our assistance, trusting that God will assist us. A weak faith benefits from renewed prayer, Scripture reading, church attendance, fasting, and almsgiving. The virtues of hope and trust can be renewed; they are not gone forever

Powerlessness relates to our extreme vulnerability. We no longer are protected from the unthinkable. We feel that we are helpless against random terrorist attacks. We feel that we are helpless against a powerful hierarchy in the Church or a falling stock market. However, this sense of powerlessness may be reckoned with when we begin to understand that while we do not have any control over random attacks, we do have control over the way we respond to them.

Denial, anger, fear, anxiety, and powerlessness, are all appropriate reactions to crisis and trauma, but they do not need to be permanent responses. In fact, the opposite is true. These responses must be neutralized and proven otherwise. Anger and anxiety must be relieved, better sooner than later, for the sake of our physical health. The key here is our resilience, our ability to bounce back. And we Americans are known to have great resilience. We have faced and overcome many, many tragedies, crises, and traumas throughout the years.

The Death of Denial and Powerlessness

Gavin de Becker is widely considered America's leading expert on predicting and managing violent behavior. He advises such clients as the CIA and the U.S. Supreme Court. His seventy-member firm has protected clients from terrorism in Israel, southern Africa, Europe, and South America. He designed the assessment systems used to screen threats to all federal judges and the governors of eleven states, and his work has changed the way the U.S. government protects its highest officials.

De Becker wrote his most recent book entitled Fear Less[18] during the six weeks immediately following September 11. He asserts from the beginning, "In this war, there will be no captured beachhead upon which we can lay our fears to rest. So we are challenged to find safety and peace of mind in new ways."

After discussing specific recommendations that can enhance our national security and our individual safety—and help put our fear into perspective—he believes that you will come to the same conclusions that he has: namely, "that you can find your life in these times, that you can influence your own safety, that you can help protect your country, that you can manage fear, and that you are going to be all right."

He quickly adds, "You can be safer and feel safer. I don't mean a fraudulent feeling made possible by denial ... I mean a true, informed feeling of safety that comes from understanding violence, risk, intuition, fear, and security."

"Americans, after all, are experts at denial," he asserts, "a choir whose song could be titled, 'Things Like That Don't Happen in This Neighborhood.'"

---

[18] Gavin de Becker, *Fear Less*; Little, Brown & Co., Boston: 2002.

He explains, "Since September 11, we've had to let go of plenty of old beliefs, so that in addition to everything else, we have experienced the death of denial. Denial is the psychological defense mechanism we unconsciously deploy to make unpleasant truths go away, but on September 11 those defenses were breached, leaving millions of people overwhelmed by terrifying ideas and feelings.

"Denial," he continues, "has an insidious side effect. For all the peace of mind deniers think they get by saying it isn't so, the fall they take when faced with new violence is all the more unsettling. Denial is a save-now/pay-later scheme . . . for in the long run the denying person knows the truth at some level, and it causes a constant low-grade anxiety."

De Becker's challenge to us is to replace denial with compartmentalization. "To compartmentalize is not to deny; it is to acknowledge the reality of something, look right at it, and place it, literally, in a mental compartment, in a kind of quarantine, separated from our moment-to-moment thinking in such a way that we can manage life. The theory here is to change what we can change and accept what we cannot change. Violence is one of those things we cannot change; it is always present. What differs is the expression of violence, but violence itself has remained a constant throughout human history.

"So, even if it's sad to think of violence as a constant," de Becker writes, "acceptance of reality is always the highest ground you can find—and the safest—because from there you can see what's coming. From there, you can evaluate risks and organize defenses. From there, you can hear the messengers of intuition, the powerful and effective force at the center of your natural survival system."

Unwarranted Fear, Worry, Anxiety

Just as de Becker considers intuition a powerful force in our survival systems, he also places fear there.

"So, of course, you've felt fear about terrorism. How could you not? Nobody could witness what you witnessed, even if through the small window of television, and not react with shock and fear. As I've reminded many victims of violence many times, your defense system is designed to send the fear signal when it perceives enormous danger–and your defense system had never before assessed anything quite like what happened on September 11, or what's been happening since.

"Should you feel fear? you ask. The question is irrelevant, for there is no *should* about fear. Of course you will feel fear *when there is reason to*, like it or not. Fear *is*, and is supposed to *be*. Start there, accept it, and give yourself some of the same compassion you've so willingly extended to others since September 11.

"Intuition has many messengers but the clearest and most urgent is fear. Nothing in life gets attention as reliably as fear–and that's the way our system is designed to work. Of course, you imagine a thousand terrors; that's where terrorism really happens—in the imagination."

De Becker provides definitions:

True fear is a signal in the presence of danger. It is always based upon something we perceive, something in our environment or our circumstance.

Unwarranted fear is always based upon our memory or our imagination.

Anxiety is caused by uncertainty which is a key component of terrorism; we are left to wonder what might happen next, to what degree, and where.

Worry is the fear we manufacture—it is not authentic, and it is not part of our defense system. Unlike fear which is involuntary, worry is a choice.

De Becker concludes this section of his book by saying "If a person feels fear constantly, there is no signal left for when it's really needed. Thus, the person who chooses to worry all the time or to persistently chew on unwarranted fears is actually making himself *less safe*. Worry is not a precaution; it is the opposite because it delays and discourages constructive action, *and action is the antidote to worry*.

"Just as your imagination has placed you in frightening situations, it is now time to place yourself in empowering situations, time to see that you have a role to play, and contrary to so many TV news stories, it isn't just victim-in-waiting."

De Becker is tough on TV newscasts which he feels have invented their own form of newspeak which distorts reality and plays on fear. He offers five "Terror-Free Guidelines".

1. Turn off the TV news.
2. Keep it off–long enough to realize that you are not missing anything and that you are actually feeling happier, more courageous, more connected to people, and, surprisingly, better informed.
3. Get your information in print. Read—especially *Time* magazine or *U.S. News & World Report* or *Newsweek*, or your local newspaper.
4. Get information. Do research. Check the Internet, go to a library, look at a Web site, ask a smart friend.
5. Talk to people in your life about world and local events.

Unforgiveness—A Major Stumbling Block

Of all the feelings named above, unforgiveness is the most serious spiritual stumbling block to the healing process. Unforgiveness prevents or prolongs healing as we enter the recovery period after some crises or disasters.

In some cases of unforgiveness, there is a stubbornness grounded in the depths of our hurt that just will not go away. "I will not forgive him under any under circumstances!" we say about an abusive spouse. "After what she did, she is the last person on this earth that I would ever consider forgiving!" we declare about a meddling mother-in-law. "Forgive Osama bin Laden?—Are you crazy?"

A father laments, "If your son spoke to you the way mine did, you would never forgive him either!" This father has been deeply hurt by his son's words said in anger and rage. The father maintains, "I would forgive him if only he took responsibility for what he said and apologizes to me! But he will not even acknowledge that he said these horrendous things to me—words no father should ever have to hear!"

The son, while mildly aware of his father's anger, figures, "He'll get over it," and goes on with his very busy life of husband, father, student, and bread-winner. Who is being hurt here? The answer is the father, of course, as his anger and hurt continue to eat away at him, contribute to high blood pressure and produce a rumbling in his stomach every time he thinks of his son.

Have you ever found it terribly difficult, or even impossible, to forgive someone? It is often most difficult to forgive those closest to us—our family and our friends.

But how do we forgive our enemies? Do we even try to forgive them? We are told to forgive our enemies. How can we forgive bin Laden or the terrorists? How can we forgive abusive priests or the bishops who have participated in the silence? How can we forgive greedy corporate executives? It's not easy to forgive them, if you've lost your life savings.

Blaming is So Much Easier

It is so much easier to blame people (and God). Blaming others serves a purpose. Blaming others often allows us to avoid facing our own responsibility. And blaming others allows us to hold people at arm's length. Once burned, twice shy! When others have hurt us, we don't *want* to get close to them, because we are afraid that they'll hurt us again.

In the same way, unforgiveness with family or friends serves a purpose. Holding a grudge allows us to hold people at arm's length. We don't *want* to forgive because we're afraid of being hurt. We say that we want intimacy; but often, we're afraid of intimacy because we've been hurt so deeply by those close to us.

But, it's not quite the same story with strangers such as bin Laden, Hitler, Hussein, and corporate executives. Some will say that they are *unable* to forgive these people. We can encourage them to forgive, but we must not rush them. It may just take time. Many people *know* (in their heads) that they need to offer forgiveness, but are unable to forgive (in their hearts).

Who Will Throw the First Stone?

Can we tie in the "which of us will throw the first stone?" with the perpetrators of these crises? The answer is "yes, but very carefully!" My daughter told me of her experience at Mass during the height of the church crisis when the homilist, speaking on the need for forgiveness of our *second* bishop to resign because of pedophilia, reminded everyone at Mass that no one is perfect. "We all have mistakes in our past, behaviors which we regret." He said. "Which of you will throw the first stone?"

She was outraged that he appeared to be comparing her and the others present with abusive priests and, in the case of our diocese, two back-to-back abusive bishops. "These are extremes," she told me. "I definitely have done things that I am not proud of in my past, but I certainly didn't abuse little children or bomb the Twin Towers! It's absurd to compare us with bin Laden or the abusive priests." I agreed with her. But, nevertheless, Jesus has asked us to consider our own sinfulness before condemning others. "Judge not that ye be not judged" (Matthew 7:1).

We know that Jesus tells us we are to forgive our enemies *"seventy times seven,"* but sometimes we need help to forgive some of these people who have caused irreparable harm, a tremendous amount of help. And asking God to help us forgive in this situation is okay! However, we should not be made to feel guilty if we cannot forgive someone yet. People have been victimized enough through all of these crises. Inappropriate guilt is the last thing any of us need!

Maybe all that some people can do at this time is acknowledge their inability to forgive or their own unwillingness even to *consider* forgiveness. Unforgiveness may be a major stumbling block, but unforgiveness can turn into forgiveness, given time. Some people just simply cannot forgive bin Laden—yet! Maybe we need to admit honestly that we cannot forgive him (or anyone else) yet. Perhaps our own awareness of our inability to forgive, our lack of forgiveness for others, will put us in touch with our own imperfections.

Specks and Planks

In the gospel of Matthew, we are reminded that to avoid judgment, we must stop passing judgment on others. *"Why look at the speck in your brother's eye when you miss the plank in your own?"*

No, it is not fair to be compared to monsters such as bin Laden. But perhaps we do need to acknowledge and own our own scandalous, ambitious or prideful behavior and seek God's mercy and forgiveness. Perhaps we need to search our own hearts *first* for any way in which we have participated, caused, or contributed to these hurtful situations? Are there times when we have looked the other way, aided and abetted, or hurt others? What about our ambition, pride, greed, and arrogance as Americans? How do we treat our own neighbors? How do we treat Arab-Americans? What about profiling? What about our own prejudices?

Soul-searching can be very beneficial, and yet we must be kind and merciful to ourselves, as God is kind and merciful to us. We need to examine our consciences regularly, but we must try to avoid sinking into the mires of inappropriate guilt. Many people, in this post-trauma period, are already dealing with too many negative emotions.

It is important for us to acknowledge our own shortcomings, weakness or failures, but we need to do this with great sensitivity for ourselves and others. In other words, we do not need to be so hard on ourselves at times when we, too, are suffering greatly.

There is no shame in admitting that we cannot forgive someone yet. It would be worse to make a pretense of forgiveness. We are talking about honesty now. As we stated from the beginning, "It's time to be honest now—with ourselves—and with God."

It is not sinful to be unable to forgive someone, either, although our unforgiveness comes back to haunt us. *Forgive us our trespasses as we forgive those who trespass against us.* We must ask ourselves if we cannot forgive yet or completely, does the same standard hold to how we want our trespasses to be forgiven—eventually and only partially? But, still, if we simply cannot yet forgive someone in our heart, then we turn to God and ask God to forgive that person for us, since we truly are unable to do so at this time. *Father, forgive them for they know not what they do.* Our God is a merciful God.

"Forgiving the Unforgivable"

Recently one of the popular women's magazines ran a story about a woman whose granddaughter was kidnapped, horribly abused and raped, murdered, and left in a garbage bin behind a restaurant. I cannot remember the exact details in the article, but the title of the article was, "Forgiving the Unforgivable." The child's murderer was found, convicted, and sentenced to death.

For the longest time, the grandmother could not even go near the restaurant where they found the child. But one day, she went to visit her pastor and told him of her horrible suffering and especially her inability to forgive the murderer. After weeks and weeks of counseling and prayer, she finally was able to forgive the man, and she found a remarkable sense of freedom and peace. She was no longer using an enormous amount of negative energy to hate this man.

Much to her surprise, she soon found herself regretting that he had been sentenced to death. She thought to herself, "Violence only begets more violence. We are doing the very thing to him that he did to my beloved grandchild!" She began to protest the death penalty for this man, but eventually he was executed.

She has gone on, though, to found a ministry which opposes the death penalty in her state. This is definitely a story of a woman who was able to "forgive the unforgivable!"

Forgiveness is a Gift

Some people may scoff at this story and say that it is impossible to forgive the perpetrator of such a crime. The loss of a child or a grandchild is one of the most painful and severe losses that a person can experience. It presents a situation so outside of the natural order of things. A child's death resulting from a long-term, incurable illness demands that we share the suffering of our child, while a violent death offers no preparation, no chance to say goodbye.

Out of my own experience, I know that forgiveness is a gift, given freely by God. When my 25-year-old son Danny was killed by a drunk driver on Christmas Day, 1994, I was immediately given the gift of forgiveness for the young man who killed him. Sheer gift. And I didn't even ask for it. It just came—in the sense of feeling tremendous pity for the driver, knowing that he would have to live with this horrible tragedy on his conscience for the rest of his life. I instantly felt pity for him and compassion for his mother, since I knew that I would find it terribly difficult if one of my children had killed one of hers. So, I received the gift of forgiveness immediately.

When this young man posted bail, he evaded the immigration officers and fled to his native Brazil which does not offer extradition for Brazilian citizens. Even then I was spared from a sense of debilitating anger or self-destructive revenge. Again, sheer gift.

At other times in my life, forgiveness has been a gift handed to me on a silver platter—and has saved me light-years of anger and wasted energy. I think of the Scripture verse, *Every good and perfect gift is from above, coming down from the Father of lights (James 1:17).* All good gifts come from God. Forgiveness certainly qualifies as a *good* gift. Ask for it!

What forgiveness is and is not:[19]

Forgiveness is an act of our free will. We do not have to feel forgiving to forgive.

Forgiveness holds others accountable for their behavior.

Forgiveness cancels the debt that someone owes me.

Forgiveness means I let go of the desire for revenge. (Anger to the point of seeking revenge or of possibly harming the other person is a sin.)

Forgiveness seeks restoration, to the extent that the other is capable of a healthy relationship.

---

[19] Joan M. Houck, *Heart Basics, p. 183. (Available toll free at 1-866-428-3463.)*

Forgiveness loves courageously, knowing that those who dare to love *will be hurt* by others.

Forgiveness frees me to get on with my life.

Forgiveness frees the other to face the ways he/she has harmed me.

Forgiveness does not ignore the hurt, or ignore painful unmet needs, or gloss over anger.

Forgiveness does not mean forgive and forget.

Forgiveness does not erase the memory of the hurt, but it gradually drains the memory of the pain surrounding the hurt.

Without forgiveness, healing and reconciliation will not occur.

Forgiving Someone: For Your Own Sake

Our inability to forgive takes its toll on us physically, emotionally and spiritually. *Not forgiving* someone takes a lot of energy! And, as we all know, we are the ones hurt by our hatred or anger. In many cases, the person we need to forgive is not even aware of our unforgiveness or for the need for forgiveness in the first place!

When we forgive someone from the heart, we often think that we are doing the other person a favor, but it is actually the other way around. We are doing ourselves a great favor! Harbored resentments, hate, hurt–even when they are justified–simply poison our own system. Festering under the surface, they become more and more painful. Eventually they come to a head and either burst or their poison spreads to other parts of our lives or bodies. Our physicians will tell us that pent-up anger often leads to stroke, heart disease, depression and self-anguish.

But, the trick is to forgive from the heart, not from the head, since the latter only leads to the same resentments and anger continuing to resurface. We think we have forgiven someone and find that, in the long run, we have come to resent them even more. And each new day or act on their part just deepens our layers of anger and resentment.

Forgiveness is an act of the will. Often forgiveness does not result in an immediate change in our feelings. However, repeated decisions to choose to forgive often result in a gradual change in our feelings toward that person. The quality of our forgiveness is not measured by our feelings, but by the firmness of our decision to forgive.

The Role of Reconciliation in Healing

Forgiveness is different from reconciliation. Forgiveness takes one person. I can forgive whether or not the other chooses to forgive, whether or not the other chooses to accept my forgiveness, and even whether or not the other person accepts responsibility for the harm done to me.

Reconciliation (in the sense of interpersonal reconciliation, not sacramental reconciliation with God), however, takes two people. I have control over whether or not I will choose to forgive. I do not have control over whether the other person takes a share of the responsibility. I do not have control over whether the other person will accept a sincere apology or, if appropriate, offer one in return. Therefore, I do not have control over whether or not reconciliation will take place.

Given this understanding of reconciliation, which I call personal reconciliation, it may never occur under certain circumstances or between specific people. For instance, if reconciliation takes two people, then you and bin Laden will never be reconciled, even if you were willing to forgive him for the horrendous attacks on the

American people. If the six million Jews who died in the holocaust and their families were able to forgive Hitler, reconciliation still would not happen.

If the hurting father forgives the ugly words of the hurtful son, reconciliation still may not occur since it depends on a mutual response from both father and son. The son may refuse to admit that he even made horrendous statements. He may not recognize his own responsibility in the argument. Therefore, in that case, reconciliation could not take place. Reconciliation is a two-way street.

Perhaps it is unrealistic to expect personal reconciliation in every case, although forgiveness and healing are always possible and attainable.

The Sweetness of Reconciliation

True reconciliation is sweet indeed. We have all had spats with our spouses, children, friends, neighbors, co-workers. How delightful it is when apologies are sincerely given *and* accepted! How extra delightful when the incidents were quite serious (not just spats)! How frightful when apologies are neither offered nor accepted!

This, also, is perhaps what makes the Sacrament of Reconciliation so sweet. When we truly repent and say we are sorry to God, there is no such thing as God dismissing or ignoring our apology. There is no such thing as long-term resentment or anger. God, the other person in this relationship, always forgives. Why? Because God loves us unconditionally. When we repent of our sins, when we say we are sorry, when we turn back to a life of pleasing God with our words, thoughts and actions, God does not reject us. He forgives us and rejoices with us.

This beauty and sweetness surrounds the story of the Prodigal Son. The father loves him unconditionally, and the fatted calf is slain for a celebratory feast. *"My son was lost, but now is found."*

Reconciliation between two humans may not always occur as we would like and may continue to be a stumbling block to our complete healing. But reconciliation with God is always possible, and necessary for healing. It is pride that prevents us from seeking reconciliation with God or for not being reconciled with God.

Reconciliation with God is a two-way street. The good news is that if you move even an inch toward reconciliation, God will meet you more than half-way and encourage you to come the rest of the way. And then the Father will dance!

Our Enemies–Far from the Limits of Compassion

Fear Less, the book by Gavin de Becker from which I have previously quoted at length, is written from a technical—not spiritual—point of view. Nevertheless, de Becker offers important spiritual principles. The expert on violent behavior writes, "Mohamed Atta may hold the top position on an awful list of mass killers, but he is not unique. He can be understood. Though it may be too early for most of us to think about forgiveness, even Mohamed Atta is not beyond the limits of our compassion. Nobody is. Being compassionate is not something we do for Atta—it is something we do in our own interest because humanizing another person is the only route to real understanding. When it comes to an enemy, understanding is required whether we want to forgive him, befriend him, or defeat him."[20]

---

[20] De Becker, op. cit., excerpts from pp.176 – 198. In his final chapter, "Far From the Limits of Compassion," de Becker provides a reasoned discussion for compassion and understanding. I wish I could reprint the entire chapter. This book is a positive, uplifting approach to healing our wounds, increasing our safety and security, and living life fully without unwarranted fear or anxiety.

After asserting that it was pain—cultural and historical pain—that was behind the acts of September 11, de Becker asks and answers a question that many Americans asked, especially when it was reported that there was dancing in the street of Baghdad on that awful day:

"Why would anyone hate us so much?

"Millions of people in the Middle East have spent their lives with the things we experienced for just a few minutes: smoke, rubble, fire, dust, instability, uncertainty, explosions. . . . By most estimates, Iraq lost more sons and brothers and fathers in twelve weeks than we lost in Vietnam in twelve years, and Iraq is a country with one-tenth our population. . . . At the start of our war and subsequent boycott against Iraq, a few hundred children younger than five were killed each month by respiratory infections, malnutrition, and diarrheal illnesses. The shameful number is now more than five thousand—*per month*. . . .

"None of what I am sharing is about right or wrong, or ideology, or politics. I know very well that America contributes enormously to millions of people around the world, and I am proud of much of what we do. In pointing out both sides of our international reputation, I have just one purpose: to answer the question of why we are hated by so many. Einstein said, 'Peace cannot be kept by force. It can only be achieved by understanding.'"

The process of healing and forgiving may seem uncertain. But one thing is certain. No matter how we feel, no matter what has happened to us, no matter what the world may tell us, we belong to God. And, as children of God, we are commanded (not requested) to pray for our enemies. As we know, it can be incredibly difficult at times.

But, when we humanize our enemies, as de Becker suggests as absolutely necessary for understanding them, then perhaps we also can feel some compassion and eventually be able to forgive them. Meanwhile, we can pray for them, especially for all of the innocent children.

A Model of Forgiveness

Perhaps we can find a model of forgiveness in the following short prayer of an unknown woman. This prayer was found on a piece of wrapping paper in the *Ravensbruck* concentration camp. She asked God to forgive her enemies. This prayer will remind us of our need to forgive others, especially our enemies, and to ask forgiveness for ourselves.

Food for Thought
A Prayer for Forgiveness of Our Enemies

"O Lord, remember not only the men and women of goodwill, but also those of ill will. But do not remember the suffering they have inflicted upon us. Remember, instead, the goodness which was brought, thanks to this suffering: Our comradeship, our loyalty, our humility; the courage, the generosity, and the greatness of heart which has grown out of this. And when they come to judgment, let all the fruits we have borne be their forgiveness. Amen." – An unknown prisoner at the Ravenbruck concentration camp.

*"There are many kinds of alms,
the giving of which helps us to obtain pardon for our sins;
but none is greater than that by which
we forgive from our heart a sin
that someone has committed against us."*
St. Augustine of Hippo

Practical Suggestions

1. Make a list of all the people, organizations, issues or anything you hold hate and resentment against. Then

make a serious effort from the heart to release those negative thoughts, attitude, or memories from your system and replace them with forgiveness.

2. Try to remember times in your life when you were ashamed of your sinful action or inaction. How did you feel in the midst of that experience? Afterwards? Did you make excuses for yourself? Did you think you were a "hopeless case" or did you have the hope that healing, reconciliation, and forgiveness were possible? Did you sense that God still loves you in spite of your behavior?

3. Consider how you would feel if you are lumped together and blamed in statements such as "All lawyers are . . . ." "All car-dealers are . . . ." "All parents . . . ." "All Arab-Americans are . . . ." If you were a priest or bishop, how do you think you would feel when you heard statements, "All priests are . . . ." or "All bishops . . . ."

4. Identify the "planks" in your own eyes.

5. Write a letter of support to a favorite priest or bishop or to your local newspaper supporting all of the wonderful priests and bishops in our Church.

6. Forgive someone. Write a letter to that person.

Prayerful Suggestions

1. Ask God to help you embrace the pain or loss of any unforgiveness you may be feeling. As you feel it, remember that other people are in pain also. Pray for them.

2. Ask God to enlighten you in terms of your own scandalous/ambitious/prideful behavior—but do not allow

yourself to sink into the mires of inappropriate guilt. Be kind to yourself, as God is kind to you.

3. In cases of grave sin, go to the Sacrament of Reconciliation. Read *Psalm 130* (Prayer for Pardon and Mercy). Memorize the first verse: *Out of the depths I cry to you, O* LORD; LORD, *hear my voice*!

4. Thank God for the prayerful, honest clergy of our Church. Thank God for the openness of the bishops. Thank God for the safety of your family. Thank God for the new awareness of corporate executives for the need for honesty in all business dealings. Pray for all.

For Reflection or Small Group Discussion:

1. Identify the stumbling blocks for healing and reconciliation that you experience. How could they be transformed into "stepping stones?" _____
_____
_____

2. Think of a time in your past when you found it very difficult to forgive someone. What were the circumstances? What happened? Did you finally forgive that person? How? What helped you to take that step?
_____
_____

3. How do you feel about forgiving Osama bin Laden, abusive priests/bishops, corporate executives? Explain. Discuss. _____
_____
_____

CHAPTER FOUR

WE CALL ON GOD'S HEALING

*"He who has health has hope;
and he who has hope has everything."*
Arab proverb

*"Vitality shows not only in the ability to persist,
but in the ability to start over."*
F. Scott Fitzgerald

Opening Prayer

God of compassion and love, we gather seeking your healing touch. You are a faithful God, responding to our needs according to your unlimited generosity. We come to you with our brokenness and woundedness; we come with our hurt—physical, emotional and spiritual; and we come with our gifts. We are confident of your love and of your desire to put back together all the broken pieces of our lives.

We ask you for comfort and consolation as we try to make sense out of a broken world, even though we know that we cannot "fix" everything or return it to the way it was. As we pick up the pieces, we ask you to bless us, the builders, as we try to build a new world. We give you praise and thanks, God our Father, for being so wonderfully and powerfully present to us, and for the movement of your Spirit in our midst. Amen.

Healing: Of What?

We need to identify what it is that we want healed, what it is that needs to be healed. In the story of the healing of Bartimaeus, Jesus asks the blind beggar, *"What do you want me to do for you?"* One might think, "Isn't it pretty obvious? He's blind. He can't see. He wants his sight restored."

Well, that is exactly what Bartimaeus actually had in mind. However, it certainly was not the only possibility. Perhaps, Bartimaeus may have adjusted very well to his blindness and really was asking for healing of arthritis or high blood pressure or headaches or maybe a sin-sick soul. But Bartimaeus answers adamantly, *"Lord, I want to see."* And we know that Bartimaeus was healed.

The Lord asks the same question of us: "What do you want me to do for you?" For what are we now seeking healing? What are we seeking generally, as a result of the terrorist attacks, the sexual abuse crisis in the Church, and the crumbling economy? And what are we seeking specifically, for our individual problems, common to the stress of ordinary lives? Earlier, we discussed the importance and need of naming our wounds and losses. As we discuss the topic of healing, let us return to these and consider them a little more deeply.

The obvious place to start is to examine the wounds of our national crises. What has been wounded? How badly? Are these wounds life-threatening? Are the wounds incurable, inoperable? Or are they treatable?

All of these crises have terribly wounded, if not destroyed, our sense of safety and security. The terrorist attacks have produced fear in terms of possible future attacks or chemical warfare. Our security and trust in the hierarchy of the Church has diminished significantly and has not yet been fully restored. For many, personal financial security is a thing of the past.

So, in essence, we have lost a great deal in the area of Safety and Security (physical safety, emotional/spiritual stability, and economic security). These are very real losses and affect all areas of our lives.

A Psychological Approach

Carl Rogers and many other psychologists agree that each person is born with a potential for growth which provides the impetus for behavior. We call this innate tendency to grow into a fully mature individual "self-actualization." This process is likened to the potential of a seed to become a flower, unless there are obstructions presented to its natural growth.

In theological terms, the potential for growth is similar. A person will innately seek to grow in holiness, which we call *sanctification*. As we grow in holiness by responding to the grace of the Holy Spirit, we can become all that God intended us to be when we were created in the first place. St. Augustine said, "Our hearts are restless until they rest in Thee." The caveat here is the same as for self-actualization. Sanctification will occur naturally unless there are obstructions presented. (Remember the stumbling blocks of the last chapter? Denial, fear, unforgiveness?)

Abraham Maslow agreed that people have this innate tendency toward growth, called self-actualization. In these theories, this innate motive accounts for all human behavior, from basic food-seeking to the most sublime acts of artistic creativity and spiritual thought.

Unlike Rogers, though, Maslow suggested that failure to realize one's full, human potential is caused by the presence of unmet needs. These needs are viewed by Maslow as forming a hierarchy (illustrated below) including the basic physiological requirements (like food and water) as well as higher-level requirements such as safety and security, love and belonging, self-esteem, and, finally self-actualization.

Maslow's Hierarchy

5. Self-Actualization
4. Self-Esteem
3. Love and Belonging
2. Personal Safety and Security
1. Basic Physiological Requirements
(Food, Water, Air)

Maslow contends that satisfaction of each need level must be preceded by the meeting of all lower-level needs. For example, one is not going to be concerned about meeting his needs for self-esteem (the fourth level) if he does not know where his next meal is coming from (a first level need) or if he wonders if his family will have a roof over its head (second level). So, according to this schema, even though we all have the potential for full actualization, that potential cannot be sought or expressed if lower-level needs remain unfulfilled.

This theory took on a new significance in the United States after September 11. Most people in the United States were *not* struggling to meet basic needs of providing food, shelter, and safety for their families unless perhaps they were well below the poverty level, homeless, or living in high crime areas. Before September 11, people had been concerned about smog and pollutants in the air. After September 11, they became acutely concerned about airborne chemical warfare.

Suddenly, they found themselves in a whole new ball game. National security had always been an important issue prior to September 11, but in relatively abstract ways.

After September 11, people for the first time were genuinely concerned with direct attacks on the United States and fear of anthrax poisoning. More than a year later, Americans are dealing with talk of widespread smallpox epidemics and preemptive strikes against Iraq. Armed guards fill the airports and some communities are distributing gas masks. People are now wondering if their food and water are safe to eat and drink.

In other words, according to Maslow, people will not be as concerned about *consciously* achieving their highest levels of spiritual potential while they are worrying about basic safety and security issues such as safe drinking water, anthrax attacks, college funding, or loss of life savings.

However, since Maslow's and the others' theories are *humanistic* theories, they do not take into account a theology of a powerful God who is attracting people to holiness and healing. Believers probably turn to God more frequently or with more urgency and a much greater need for aid and protection in the time of crisis. The same might be said of unbelievers. ("There are no atheists in foxholes.") If these crises result in people running into the everlasting arms of God, that will be a welcome result. Then, the burden will be on the churches in America to provide follow-up to help people stay on their journey to healing and wholeness.

Where is God in All of This?

On the other hand, people suffering from fear of terrorism or economic crisis or whatever may fear that God has abandoned them. "Where is God in all of this?" is a common question. These fears, or doubts, or sense of disbelief, wondering, or questioning are valid in that they are real in the minds of those people experiencing them. We must not discount these fears of abandonment or doubt. Theologian Paul Tillich tells us, "Doubt is not the opposite of faith but an integral part of faith." Luis Evely writes in his book, *Suffering*, "Doubt is the beginning of faith." While these fears of abandonment are valid, nothing could be further than the truth. It is impossible that God would ever abandon us. God has promised us that he would never leave us.

Recently, Bishop Sean Patrick O'Malley, OFM Cap., was installed in the Diocese of Palm Beach. In his homily, he remarked, "Where is it in the Gospels that Jesus says: If you follow me, you will make lots of money, you will eat well and never get high cholesterol, and you will win the lottery at regular intervals? I have searched for that illusive passage and never seem to find it. Actually Jesus never promised us that nothing would go wrong; he promised us that he would be with us: *I will be with you always, even to the end of the world.*"

Bishop O'Malley repeated, "Christ never promised that nothing would go wrong, but he promised to be with us. He needs us to be faithful and faith-filled. The present Church crisis calls us to redress wrongs of the past, to repent of our sins and errors, but also calls us to a profound spiritual conversion to move into the future."

Acceptance—A Choice

For many of us, there are now irreversible losses which no amount of faith, short of miracles, can reverse in this world. The world as we knew it simply no longer exists. We cannot return to yesterday or yesteryear.

Some of us have experienced irreversible losses such as the death of a spouse or a child. Some of us have seen a marriage die or lose their good health. In order for emotional and spiritual healing to occur, we must accept the reality of our loss. This is what the grieving process is all about. It is not until we can acknowledge the reality and accept the finality of our losses that we can choose to move on.

Healing is a choice. We can choose to recover and regain our strength after traumatic life events. Or we can choose to remain in the ashes, licking our wounds. For example, I remember the woman who came to me shortly after my son died and said, "I know exactly how you feel. I have cried every day since my own son died. I can't even go to work. I just weep and weep every time I visit his grave, and I have not missed going to the cemetery for even one single day . . . for the past fourteen years!" No, she did not know exactly how I felt!

Time heals. This is true, unless we choose to keep the wound open and festering, as this poor woman did. She chose to focus on death. God urges us to focus on life. We have the assurance that God journeys with us in our pain and in our sadness. Our faith allows us to survive, to live *through*, to live *with* the pain, the mystery, the loss—and come out on the other side—Resurrection! *"Life has not ended; it has changed."*

God told us: *"Here, then, I have today set before you life and prosperity, death and doom. . . . I have set before you life and death, the blessing and the curse. Choose life, then that you and your descendants may live, by loving the Lord, your God, heeding his voice and holding fast to him. For that will mean life for you, a long life for you...."* (*Deut.* 30:15, 19-20).

Acceptance is necessary for our spiritual and emotional healing, as individuals and as a nation. But acceptance is not denial. Acceptance is openly acknowledging the facts that: yes, the world is no longer the same; yes, the Church is no longer the same; yes, the economy is no longer the same. With this knowledge and acceptance, we can move on. We can make adjustments to accommodate a new and changing world. We can choose to investigate different attitudes concerning the hierarchy. We can choose to modify our lifestyles.

Perhaps herein lies the wisdom of the *Serenity Prayer* lies—in knowing what changes we can make, what changes we cannot make, and having the wisdom to know the difference. Life will not be the same, but it will be *life*. It will be different. But with a God of love and mercy beside us, it can be *life to the full*.

The Healing of Our Nation

We must look not only to our individual healing, but to the healing of the nation. In the last chapter, we were reminded to look for the *"planks in our own eyes"*: ambition, pride, greed, arrogance, prejudices, injustice, weak faith. Someone, somewhere, somehow, must have the courage to call the entire nation to accountability.

The President of the United States wrote, "We have been the recipients of the choicest bounties of heaven. We have been preserved, these many years, in peace and prosperity. We have grown in numbers, wealth and power, as no other nation has ever grown. But we have forgotten God.

"We have forgotten the gracious hand which preserved us in peace, and multiplied and enriched and strengthened us; and we have vainly imagined, in the deceitfulness of our hearts, that all these blessings were produced by some superior wisdom and virtue of our own.

"Intoxicated with unbroken success, we have become too self-sufficient to feel the necessity of redeeming and preserving grace, too proud to pray to the God that made us! It behooves us, then to humble ourselves before the offended Power, to confess our national sins and to pray for clemency and forgiveness." These words written by President Abraham Lincoln in 1863 still resonate today.

The Role of Sacraments and Prayer in Healing

We have many resources in the Church to help us through the healing process: sacraments, scripture, prayer, the community of believers.

The Sacrament of Reconciliation is extremely beneficial in the healing of anger, resentment, and sinfulness. Without forgiveness (individually and nationally), healing and salvation can not occur. (The root word of salvation is *salve*, as in salve that we put on a wound and is used in the process of healing.)

The Sacrament of Eucharist and the Sacrament of the Sick are also extraordinary spiritual tools in the process of healing. With Eucharist, we are strengthened for the journey with the bread of heaven, the Body and Blood of Jesus Christ, our Lord and Savior. And with the Sacrament of the Sick, we are gently and mercifully blessed and anointed specifically for healing.

"Soaking prayer" is a term for constant, continual, on-going prayer for an individual and is usually utilized by a group of like-minded believers for the healing of a very specific condition or illness. Communal prayers are offered during liturgies for the sick of the parish. Private prayers and intercession of saints also are efficacious routes to healing.

Sacraments work. Prayer works. I am reminded of a priest friend of mine who was called to the hospital shortly after his ordination to anoint a dying woman in the hospital. The doctors and family had given up hope; the woman was in a coma. The priest celebrated the Sacrament of the Anointing of the Sick for the very first time, with her family surrounding her bed. Lo and behold, by the next morning the woman was sitting up in bed, chatting with her amazed doctors and family. The priest was overcome with surprise: "It worked!" he proclaimed to all. (This is a true story. This priest went on to establish a nationally acclaimed healing ministry. Part of his gift of healing, he would say, was that his first experience with the Sacrament led him to *expect* people to be healed!) I have witnessed with my own eyes people whom God healed at these services—for example, the little deaf girl who then could hear and the elderly priest confined to a wheel chair with MS who pushed his chair out of the auditorium after the service. I have read about thousands of completely documented healings.

God does heal! God does work miracles in this day and age. But there is no formula for why God heals some and not others. At times, I have heard some very bad theology. For instance, I have heard it said that "all we need for God to heal us is enough faith." I have heard disappointed patients say that "God must not love me as much as the other people who were healed." I have heard them also say, "My faith must not be strong enough." So many "excuses" are offered for why some are healed and others are not. The truth is that we do not know why some are not healed. I believe that these are the mysterious occasions when we will not have the answers and we need to allow God to be God.

Healing does not depend on our faith; it depends on God's power. God chose to heal the centurion's servant, and he had no religious faith at all, but he did trust in the authority of Jesus. Jesus later remarked, "He had more trust than all of the Israelites."

Sacraments and prayer are very positive roads leading to healing. Even if miraculous healing does not occur, we have the healing presence of God in our midst, in our mind, in our memory.

The Power of Scripture in Healing

Sticks and stones may break my bones, but names can never hurt me is the old childhood rhyme we learned to recite when people were being mean to us. The problem with the rhyme is that it is not true. Names and labels can seriously affect children for a lifetime.

However, Scripture also can affect a child's entire future. I remember memorizing Bible verses from an early age in the Presbyterian Sunday School which I attended. I know the power of the remembered Word of God. Even today, I can quote from memory passages which offer comfort and consolation: *The* LORD *is my Shepherd; I shall not want* . . . . When in need of encouragement, the words, *With God, all things are possible* spring up without conscious thought. When in doubt, the Word comes forth automatically: *Behold, I am with you always, even unto the end of the world.* When confusion reigns, *My ways are high above your ways...*

The words from *Isaiah 49* changed my life profoundly when I began to realize and appropriate God's unconditional love for me as a person, as an individual, as a child of God. *Can a mother forget her infant, be without tenderness for the child of her womb? Even should she forget, I will never forget you. See, upon the palms of my hands I have written your name.*

My all time favorite Scripture passage is from Jeremiah 29: 11-14: *For I know well the plans I have in mind for you, says the* LORD, *plans for your welfare, not for woe! Plans to give you a future full of hope. When you call me, when you go to pray to me, I will listen to you. When you look for me, you will find me. Yes, when you seek me with all your heart, you will find me with you, says the* LORD, *and I will change your lot!*

Much of my life and ministry have been inspired by these powerful words that assure me that God is in control. The publishing company which I started was named in honor of this prophet: Jeremiah Press. God always knows what is going on when I can't see at all; God assures me of a rainbow when all I can see is a storm.

Some of my other favorite verses are:

> *"I have not come to give you a spirit of fear, but a spirit of sound mind."*
> *"I have loved you with an everlasting love."*
> *"Whoever eats of my flesh and drinks of my blood will have eternal life."*
> *"I have come to give you life to the full."*
> *"He, who rejects you, rejects me and the One who sent me."*
> *"The Father and I are one, and we shall come and dwell within you."*

I had memorized *Psalm 23* in childhood, and to this day, I repeat it when I am feeling frustrated, frazzled, or fearful. Another favorite little story of mine revolves around this psalm, and I find the punch line so true.

Little Johnny was in the fourth grade, and the entire class was required to memorize the 23rd Psalm. All of the children worked very hard in preparation for the big day when they each would recite it for their parents. When that day came, each child stood up proudly and recited the relatively short six verses. And then it was Johnny's turn. He stumbled. He stuttered. He hemmed and hawed, even with his teacher's gentle prompting and prodding. Finally, in a strong, clear voice, he announced, "The LORD is my shepherd and that's enough for me!"

"The Lord Is My Shepherd"
A Reflection Illustrating the Word of God as Active, Alive, and Life-Changing
The LORD is my shepherd; I shall not want.
Jesus is enough for all of us; he is all that we need. This might sound like a cliché, but it is true. It is in our relationship with Jesus that we find peace, joy, hope, love, commitment, trust, and freedom from unnecessary anxiety, from unwarranted fear, from "manufactured" worry. It is our relationship with Jesus that makes our suffering and

pain tolerable; it is our relationship with Jesus that turns our weeping into laughter, our tears into smiles, our mourning into dancing. It is in our relationship with Jesus that we are healed. (*"Oh, Lord, I am not worthy; say but the word and my soul shall be healed."*)

Why is it that our relationship with Jesus is so important, you ask? The answer to this is both simple and complex. It is because we know who we are and *whose* we are. Okay, you say, "We are Christians and we belong to God. But that doesn't take the fear/anxiety/pain away." And you are right. God is not an instant cure for anything. Neither is God a "crutch for the masses," nor a mere panacea. But when we are *in* relationship with God, we are never alone. Jesus is our constant companion through the power of the Holy Spirit who dwells within us.

A mature relationship with God may take many, many years to develop, or it may develop quickly. All is grace. A friend of mine, Rob, was only 24 when he was diagnosed with leukemia. Unfortunately, a family member could not be found for the necessary bone marrow transplant. The wisdom and knowledge of skilled physicians and his youth and strength all contributed to allow Rob to be survive a blood marrow transplant from a non-related donor. What is it that kept him and his family sane during those terrible months of chemotherapy and radiation? His faith.

At an early age, Rob had developed a trusting relationship with God, and it matured very quickly with the diagnosis of cancer of the blood. Rob was blessed because he had already established a life-giving, love-giving relationship. Rob knew without a doubt that God loved him unconditionally . . . and forever . . . and before he was born . . . and eternally. Does that mean that Rob never had doubts or worries or fears? Of course not. He and his parents, aunts, uncles, sisters, and brothers all feared for his very life. But, Rob and his parents and family also had the inner assurance that God loved Rob so much that he had given his own son for him. What greater friend could Rob have?

Other people take great courage from Rob's story. He shares his journey at every opportunity and has gone on to write a wonderful book, *Coming To Terms With The Potter*[21]. It documents his entire experience including the absolute disbelief and denial that he, a healthy and athletic young adult, could be so sick at such a young age. His book also reflects the peace he has to this day, knowing that he is held securely in the palm of his best friend's hand.

> *"He makes me to lie down in green pastures*
> *and gives me rest;*
> *He leads me beside still waters*
> *and refreshes my soul.*
> *He guides me in right paths*
> *For his name's sake.*

He leads me . . . .

Have you ever wondered why your life has taken certain unplanned turns in the road? Coincidental events? Fate? Predestination? Or God's plan? In my "all-time favorite Scripture passage," God speaks clearly to us through the prophet. I believe that God truly does have *"a plan in mind for us, a plan for our welfare not for woe, for a future full of hope (Jer.29:14).*

There was a time in my life when I was floundering, searching for deeper meaning in my very ordinary life. Yet I saw only confusion. I sought the Lord, and he answered me. I kept thinking, there has to be more to life than just this. The old Peggy Lee tune came into my mind, *Is That All There Is?*

---

[21] Robert Christopher Brown, *Coming to Terms with the Potter*, Ulon Press, Fairfax, Va. 2002.

I remembered a Scripture verse that I had memorized as a child, *"Behold, I stand knocking at the door of your house. If anyone hears me calling, I will enter his home and have supper with him, and he with me* (Rev. 3:20)." In remembering this verse, though, I substituted the word "heart" for house, and realized that God was knocking on the door of my heart right then. I said, "Come in!" And he did. And we have been sharing suppers ever since—sometimes suppers of celebration, or anniversary parties, or the birth and baptismal feasts of children and grandchildren; at other times, the solitary suppers with a loved one in the hospital, a private supper between husband and wife, a funeral reception.

My life has never been the same since that day, and I have found myself on an adventure of which I had never dreamed in my wildest imagination. Of course, my life still has up's and down's, but I am never alone. He leads me.

"He guides me..."

One day while I was sitting at a traffic light that had turned red, I heard the Lord say, "Go!" No, he didn't mean for me to run the red light; he meant for me to go to a conference that I had read about a few weeks before in our diocesan newspaper. I was amazed, since it had been several weeks since I had even thought about this conference.

It was a conference on "Catholic evangelization!" *"No way,"* I said to myself as I read the announcement. *"Catholics don't evangelize. That's something that only Protestants do,"* recalling my younger years. As I recalled the article, God repeated, "Go!" And so I did.

Father Alvin Illig, CSP, had a dream, a vision, based on Pope Paul VI's historic exhortation, *"Evangelii Nuntiandi,"* or, in English, "The Gospels Must Be Proclaimed." Fr. Illig served as the first Chairman of the U.S. Bishops' Committee on Evangelization and was the founder of the Paulist National Catholic Evangelization

Association. One of his earliest efforts in the field was to design a "Lay Celebration of Catholic Evangelization," inviting lay people to come. Of course, priests were welcome, too, but the emphasis was on Catholic laity sharing their faith. *"Unheard of!"* I thought to myself. Need I say more? The rest is history, and my life truly has never been the same. After attending that 1979 conference, I took God's commandment to "go out and make disciples of all peoples" seriously. God provided the energy and enthusiasm. (Did you know that the very word *enthusiasm* means "God within us?")

"He leads me . . . He guides me?" You bet. For me, the whole wonderful, hectic, zany world of Catholic evangelization included being a jet-set circuit rider as I preached parish missions in the United States, Canada, Europe, and the Caribbean. Although that never quite qualified as "green pastures or still waters," God very definitely restored my soul and refreshed my spirit. And I have found that when I do need "green pastures and still waters" to rest and recover, he provides them for me, sometimes in the most unexpected ways. For example, I recall the weeklong silent retreat I spent in a tree house overhanging the quiet waters of a gently running stream in the mountains of Western Massachusetts—what a treat! But most of the time my life is busy and sometimes hectic. Then I find the *"green pastures and still waters"* deep in my heart, where I am refreshed by the peace of the Holy Spirit.

"Even though I walk in the valley of the shadow of death . . . I will fear no evil; for you are at my side. Your rod and your staff give me courage."

"The valley of the shadow of death . . ." sure sounds like a scary place, doesn't it? It is. Many of us have been there as we experienced the suffering and death of parents, children, friends, spouses. Or, we experienced it while helplessly watching as a young person abandons all that he

or she has become and turns his or her life over to the power of drugs. Some have struggled with the death of hopes and dreams in separation or divorce proceedings. Some struggle with the battle of making ends meet. We watch in pain as friends suffer losses and sorrow. We recoiled in horror when the Twin Towers were attacked.

We have either already been in the "valley of the shadow of death" or we will be there at some time in our life. But the Lord's rod and staff are there to comfort us, to protect and defend us, to prod us on, to head us in the right direction, and to surround us with caring brothers and sisters in the Lord. We are never alone. God gives us the courage and strength to do what we have to do, to be who we have to be for others.

I know this from personal experience. When my youngest son died so tragically, God quickly stepped in with his rod and his staff. They not only comforted me, but protected and defended me from the evil one. I was protected from breakdown, from despair, and from all of the "What ifs?" and "If onlys?"

An especially wonderful blessing came the night before Danny's funeral as our family sat together in the dim lights of the Christmas tree. His unopened presents under the tree poignantly reminded us of our son and brother. Did anyone have any unfinished business? Was there anything said or done that we regretted or wished we could take back? Were angry words exchanged? We sat in silence for awhile, deep in thought. Amazingly, none of the eight of us had any regrets except a common one: we didn't have a chance to say goodbye to Danny!

After the first shock of seeing three police officers on my doorstep very early on that Christmas morning, I experienced an incredible sense of peace and calm throughout all of the funeral preparations and even the funeral itself. I remember asking my priest friend if it was possible to go through all five stages of grief at once and immediately arrive at the final stage of acceptance? (He told me, "No," and he was right in the long run.)

At that time, I was comforted and prodded by my shepherd's rod and his staff. God gave me the strength and the courage to do what I needed to do, to be who I needed to be, while others around me were grief-stricken and barely functioning in both shock and denial. Eventually, of course, the tremendous sadness and grief hit me months later in a delayed reaction. And that was when the Lord led me once again into green pastures and beside the still waters. I was never alone.

> *"You prepare a banquet before my enemies,*
> *You anoint my head with oil;*
> *My cup runneth over . . . ."*

Here the shepherd turns from being a lonely shepherd to function as a generous host. In spite of danger and disruption, Jesus supplies me with a generous meal, a banquet! With enemies raging nearby, he says, "Come, sit down. Let me nourish you; let me feed you; let me delight and surprise you with my generosity." And he does.

I experience God's generosity as I recall my very first banquet at the Table of the Lord, my own conversion experience, the sweetness of children and grandchildren, the love of my husband, the incredible life God has given us, and the incredible gift of eternal life that he has given to all of us.

And then the shepherd anoints my head with a perfumed ointment frequently used at banquets back in biblical days. God doesn't just put a dab of oil on my forehead. He takes a handful and rubs my forehead and temples when I have a headache, or massages the back of my neck when I have a stiff neck. Like a mother rubbing her child's congested chest with camphorated oil, God anoints us wherever it is needed—our heads, our hands, our hearts.

The oil is warm and feels lush and luxurious. How grateful we are!

Our cups truly do *"runneth over."* We have been given more than we could ever ask for or hope for. We had no idea of the depth of God's love for us. We cannot even begin to count all of our many blessings; they are more numerous than the stars in the sky or the grains of sand on the beach. When asked to make a list of everything we are grateful for, we run out of paper before we are even half finished. Our gratitude becomes part of the healing process in our lives. Our cups are filled again and again— *in good measure, pressed down, shaken together, running over —* abundantly!

"And surely goodness and mercy shall follow us all the rest of our life"

Wow! What an awesome promise! Do we think that God really means that? Almost sounds too good to be true, doesn't it? God works in strange and mysterious ways. Goodness and mercy are the result.

Does that mean that life is now going to be a rose garden, or as my new bishop stated it, that we will "win the lottery on a regular basis?" Well, I doubt the part about the lottery, but maybe the rose garden part will be true, as long as we remember that there are still thorns on the rose bushes. In spite of the thorns, we will see the delicate first blush of the petal and smell the sweet fragrance. Our God is with us! Emmanuel!

This does not mean that we can avoid all harm or unhappiness or disappointment or even disaster. However, we now know for certain that with God leading us, surely goodness and mercy shall follow. It cannot be any other way, in spite of the storm clouds or flying arrows.

Imagine, for a moment, that you are totally surrounded by an invisible cloud which has millions and millions of particles of goodness and mercy. The *Good*

News is that God is not just *with* us, but God is *for* us. God is on our side, no matter what the task, challenge, disaster, tragedy, or crisis. Do not be afraid!

I realized just how much of a difference it makes to have this sense of being surrounded with mercy and goodness when I went back to school at the age of forty with knees knocking and palms sweating. One of the first things my professors told me as I began the pursuit of my master's degree in pastoral ministry was, "We're on your side! We want you to do well, to succeed, to excel!" This was the opposite of my experience with some of my undergraduate professors who seemed to be out to get us, to fool us with trick questions, and to overload us with assignments to the point of physical and mental exhaustion. What a blessed relief to learn that my new teachers were cheering us on! They encouraged me to fulfill a dream that I had had since I was in high school—to earn a doctorate. I never would have succeeded if these new teachers had not been so affirming.

And that is exactly what God does with us now. God cheers us on to victory, a victory which we know is ours because it has already been won for us on the cross.

". . . *and we shall live in the house of the* LORD *forever.*"

Many years ago on a Sunday in June, I remember standing in the back of the church, a Eucharistic minister awaiting the procession. The priest, speaking to the congregation before Mass, announced, "We received a letter from a family in Wyoming which needs some help." Bob, a thirty-nine year-old high school football coach, was suffering from Lou Gehrig's disease. His parish had gathered enough money to fly Bob and his wife Judy to Boca Raton, where an experimental clinic was finding some success with a particular treatment for the deadly disease. The problem was that they needed a place for Bob and Judy to stay for the six weeks' trial treatment.

At the end of Mass, my family greeted me outside the church and asked, "Are you thinking what we are?" The decision to offer this couple our home for six weeks had already been made, simultaneously and without discussion! We were about to leave on a four-week camping trip through the Northeast, so our home and car would be available to them for at least four weeks of the trial period. They came the day we left. After short introductions and a few instructions on how to work the security system, we were gone.

At that point, Bob had great difficulty with speech. Judy told me that she had to be there with him in order to feed him, shave him, and so forth. He had very little control of his hands and arms, although he could still walk by himself.

After four weeks away, we returned to find Bob's condition somewhat improved. He had more control of his hands, and his speech came much easier. Our new friends, Bob and Judy, affected our entire community. They shared their gifts of faith, love, and hope; of humility, laughter, and pain; of suffering, acceptance, and service. They had so many gifts which they freely shared with our friends, our prayer group, and our parish.

They went to morning Mass each day and attended our weekly parish prayer meetings where all of our friends had welcomed them. So, it was natural to have a farewell party for Bob and Judy the night before they returned to Cheyenne. Unknown to all of us, they also brought the gift of music. There was not a dry eye in the house when Bob asked for a guitar and slowly began to strum with fingers that a few weeks earlier could not hold a razor. Bob sang with slightly slurred words, but with a very strong voice, *How Great Thou Art.*

We never saw Bob and Judy again. While Bob experienced improvement with the experimental treatments, they were only temporarily successful. Bob eventually received the supreme healing and his suffering was over. We truly had *"entertained angels without knowing it."* At Mass, I think of Bob when we say, *". . . and of all the angels . . . ."* and I think of Judy when we say, *". . . and of all the saints."* And I think of Judy when I think of *goodness* and I think of Bob when I think of *mercy*.

Their faith impacted my life and the lives of our entire faith community. They had many gifts which they shared openly with us and led us closer to God. It made me realize that we all have gifts that we must share freely and generously with others as we continue on the path to wholeness and holiness.

Bob and Judy remain a part of the fabric of my life and of my faith. And *surely goodness and mercy shall follow us all and we will all live in the house of the LORD forever. Amen.*

In a nutshell, this reflection illustrates what I call the "Seven Gifts of the Spirit of Healing":
1. Relationship—He is all I need.
2. Guidance—He leads me.
3. Peace—Green pastures, still waters.
4. Comfort—His rod and his staff.
5. Generosity—A banquet and anointing.
6. Assurance—Goodness and mercy.
7. Eternal life—Live in the house of the Lord forever.

What Gifts Do We Share?

My friends Bob and Judy brought their gifts of faith and love and hope and even music to share with our whole community. What gifts will we share to heal our family, our friends, our parish, our Church, our world?

The story is told of the king who invited everyone in the kingdom to an enormous feast. He asked each of the invited guests to bring only one thing: a small flask of wine that would be added to the large vats and would be shared with everyone.

On the night of the banquet, one man held his empty flask in his hand and wondered to himself, "What if I just fill it with water instead of wine? Surely, with such a large number of guests bringing wine for the vats, no one will notice. My small amount of wine surely will not make a difference."

Often we may feel like this man. We may think to ourselves, "Our small gifts will not make a difference. Surely no one will notice."

Much to the surprise of the guest bringing the water in his flask, all of the other guests did the same. Each one thought, "My small gift surely will not make a difference." Instead of sharing their small gifts of wine, there was no wine shared at all.

What will each of us bring in our flasks to heal a hurting world?

For healing and reconciliation to occur in this changing world of ours, the first step is to name our hurts and woundedness (individually and as a nation). Secondly, we need to recognize and overcome the stumbling blocks to the healing process. Thirdly, we must acknowledge the abundance of gifts from God to help us in the healing process: time, patience, presence, relationship, guidance, comfort, generosity, assurance, eternal life, forgiveness, hope, prayer, sacraments, Scripture, each other.

And we must acknowledge the abundance of gifts (an endless list) that God has given us personally to *use*, to share with others. We acknowledge our gratefulness for the many blessings we have, offering our prayers of gratitude and praise to God. We offer our gifts to God, to the Church, to the world, and, most of all, to each other. Our gifts, large or small, do make a difference. Our gifts to each other (and to ourselves) will help us heal.

FOOD FOR THOUGHT
"Stronger than all the evils in the soul is the Word, and the healing power that dwells in him."
Origen of Alexandria

Psalm 23
1) The LORD is my shepherd; I shall not want.
2) In verdant pastures he gives me repose;
   Beside restful waters he leads me;
3) He refreshes my soul.
   He guides me in right paths for his name's sake.
4) Even though I walk in the dark valley
   I fear no evil; for you are at my side
   With your rod and your staff that give me courage.
5) You spread the table before me
   in the sight of my foes;
   You anoint my head with oil;
   My cup overflows.
6) Only goodness and kindness follow me
   all the days of my life;
   And I shall dwell in the house of the LORD
   for years to come.

What Do We Want From The Lord?

What is it that we are looking for? Like Bartimaeus, what do we want from the Lord? You may want to check off some items on these lists or add your own desires.

National Healing:
    1. Justice

2. Freedom from fear
3. Release from anxiety
4. Restored confidence
5. Restored trust
6. Courage
7. Resilience
8. Joy
9. Peace of mind
10. Peace of heart
11. Peace of soul
12. Peace of spirit

Personal Healing:
1. Healing of physical illness
2. Healing of relationships
3. Recovery in chemical abuse situations
4. Strength to do what we need to do
5. Healing of mental, emotional illness
6. Acceptance
7. Resilience—ability to bounce back
8. Wisdom
9. Peace of mind
10. Peace of heart
11. Peace of soul.
12. Peace of spirit.

Practical Suggestions:

1. Write down the specifics of what you are seeking from the Lord at this time in your life. Define the healing that you are seeking.

2. Recall times when sacraments, prayer or scripture played a big part in healing in your life or others'.

3. What is your favorite Scripture? Why?

4. Speak to someone who needs healing in his or her life. Encourage them. Pray with them.

Prayerful Suggestions:

1. Ask God to help you come to accept the areas in your life that need healing. Pray to God for your healing.
2. Pray for healing of others.
3. Memorize Psalm 23.
4. Thank God for the healing that has already occurred in your life and in the lives of those close to you.

For Reflection or Discussion:

1. Think of a time in your past when you were in need of healing. What were the circumstances? What happened? Were you healed in the way that you thought you would be? How? Or, were you healed in another, unexpected area in your life?

_____
_____
_____
_____
_____
_____

2. List the people, situations, organizations, or issues in your life that are distressing. Discuss, if you are comfortable doing so.

_____
_____
_____
_____
_____
_____

3. What do you need to do for healing to occur in those situations or with those people?

_____
_____

4. When have you called on God in distress? How were you answered?

5. What areas of injustice do you "see" in your family, neighborhood, parish, community? How did you become aware of these injustices? How can you help others become aware of them? What can you do to correct them? What is one first step?

6. What gifts do you bring to the healing process?

Using Our Gifts in the Healing and Recovery Process

We all have unique gifts and talents that we can offer in the recovery process. Take a few minutes to consider the gifts or spiritual tools that you can use to help facilitate the healing and recovery process. You might want to underline the specific gifts you can utilize in the recovery/restoration phase of healing the wounds of our changing world. Underline the gifts God has given you and add additional gifts to the list.

1. Action, Alms-giving, Acceptance
2. Belief, Benevolence
3. Commitment, Constancy, Compassion Courage, Character
4. Dedication, Determination
5. Enthusiasm, Energy, Emptiness
6. Faith, Freedom, Fasting, Forgiveness
7. Goodness, Godliness
8. Honesty, Humor, Humility
9. Integrity, Intelligence
10. Justice, Joy
11. Knowledge, Kindness
12. Love, Laughter, Listening, Letting go
13. Mercy, Money
14. Neighborliness, Nobility, Nurture
15. Outlook, Openness
16. Peace, Positiveness, Possessions, Protection, Prayer
17. Questions, Quietness, Quietude
18. Relationships, Riches
19. Sacraments, Sensitivity, Sacrifices
20. Tenderness, Tolerance
21. Understanding, Uniqueness
22. Vision, Virtue
23. Watchfulness, Wisdom

24. X-cellence, X-hilaration, X-perience
25. Youthfulness, Yourself
26. Zeal, Zest

Alternate Listing of Charisms[22]

This is another list of gifts that you can examine to see which ones you possess. Determine which ones may apply toward the healing and recovery necessary in the lives of individuals, the community, and the Church.

1) The **Charism of Administration** empowers a Christian to be an effective channel of God's wisdom by providing the planning and coordination needed to accomplish good things.

2) The **Charism of Belief** empowers a Christian to be most fulfilled and spiritually fruitful by believing, for the sake of Christ, even when belief seems impossible.

3) The **Charism of Craftsmanship** empowers a Christian to be an effective channel of God's goodness to others through artistic or creative work that beautifies and/or orders the physical world.

4) The **Charism of Discernment** empowers a Christian to be an effective channel of God's wisdom by accurately perceiving and presenting to others truthful perceptions in the midst of dilemma.

5) The **Charism of Encouragement** empowers a Christian to be an effective channel of God's love—nurturing others

---

[22] This list was adapted from *"The Charisms"* as described by Sherry Weddell who founded the *"Called and Gifted Workshop: Equipping Parishes to Form Lay Apostles,"* published by the Catherine of Siena Institute.

through his or her presence and words of comfort, encouragement, and counsel.

6) The Charism of **Evangelization** empowers a Christian to be an effective channel of God's love by sharing the faith with others in a way that draws them to become disciples of Jesus and responsible members of his Church.

7) The **Charism of Faith** empowers a Christian to be an effective agent of God's purposes through an unusual trust in the love, power, and provision of God and a remarkable freedom to act on this trust.

8) The **Charism of Giving** empowers a Christian to be a cheerful channel of God's provision by giving with exceptional generosity to those in need.

9) The **Charism of Healing** empowers a Christian to be a channel of God's love through whom God cures illness and restores health when healing is unlikely to occur quickly or to happen at all.

10) The **Charism of Helping** empowers a Christian to be a channel of God's goodness by using his or her talents and charisms to enable other individuals to serve God and people more effectively.

11) The **Charism of Hospitality** empowers a Christian to be a generous channel of God's love by warmly welcoming and caring for those in need of food, shelter, and friendship.

12) The **Charism of Intercessory Prayer** empowers the intense prayer of a Christian for others to be the means by which God's love and deliverance reaches those in need.

13) The **Charism of Knowledge** empowers a Christian to be a channel of God's truth through diligent study and intellectual activity that enables us to better understand God, ourselves, and the universe.

14) The **Charism of Leadership** empowers a Christian to be an agent of God's purposes by sharing a compelling vision of a better future with others and by directing the overall efforts of a group as they work together to make the vision a reality.

15) The **Charism of Mercy** empowers a Christian to be a channel of God's love through practical deeds of compassion that relieve the distress of those who suffer and help them experience God's love.

16) The **Charism of Missionary** empowers a Christian to be a channel of God's goodness to others by effectively and joyfully using their charisms in a second culture.

17) The **Charism of Music** empowers a Christian to be a channel of God's creative goodness to others through writing or performing music for the delight of others and the praise of God.

18) The **Charism of Pastoring** empowers a Christian to be an effective channel of God's love and to build Christian community by nurturing the relationships and long-term spiritual growth of a group.

19) The **Charism of Prophecy** empowers a Christian to be a channel of divine truth and wisdom by communicating a word or call of God to individuals or a group through inspired words or actions.

20) The **Charism of Service** empowers a Christian to be a channel of God's purposes by recognizing the logistical gaps or unmet needs that can prevent good things from happening, and by personally doing whatever it takes to solve the problem and meet the need.

21) The **Charism of Teaching** empowers a Christian to be a channel of God's truth and wisdom by enabling others to learn information and skills that help them reach their fullest spiritual and personal potential.

22) The **Charism of Voluntary Poverty** empowers a Christian to be a channel of God's loving presence by living a life of cheerful, voluntary simplicity or poverty in order to identify with Jesus and the poor.

23) The **Charism of Wisdom** empowers a Christian to be a channel of God's goodness through remarkable insight that enables him or her to come up with creative solutions to specific problems and make good decisions.

24) The **Charism of Writing** empowers a Christian to be a channel of God's creativity by using words to create works of truth or beauty that reflect the fullness of human experience and bring glory to God.

CHAPTER FIVE

INSTRUMENTS OF CHANGE

"It is the action, not the fruit of the action that is important. You have to do the right thing. It may not be in your power, may not be in your time, that there will be any fruit. But that doesn't mean you stop doing the right thing. You may never know what results come from your action. But if you do nothing, there will be no result."
Mahatma Gandhi

Opening Prayer

Gracious God, Father of all, empower us with the courage, the wisdom, and the zeal to go forth and share the healing power of your Son with others. Restore our confidence in you. Help us to rebuild the world in faith as a "City of God."

Help us to remember always that we are living stones in the Kingdom and that the only firm foundation upon which we can build our lives and our very existence is your Son, Jesus Christ, the Cornerstone, our hope, our joy.

Send forth your spirit. Renew the face of the earth. Amen.

The legend is told of the rabbi and the soap maker's conversation while taking a walk. "Why is it, Rabbi," the soap maker asked, "that with so much religion, there is so much hatred in the world?"

As they walked, they passed a little orphan girl sitting at the side of the road. She was filthy dirty.

Now it was the rabbi's turn to ask a question. "Why is it, Soapmaker, that with so much soap in the world there is such dirt and filth?"

The soap maker exclaimed, "But, Rabbi, the soap must be *used* in order to eliminate the dirt!"

Throughout our lives, we have been blessed by God. Now we are invited to go forth to share that blessing with others, as facilitators of restoration, recovery, hope, and joy. In other words, we are instructed to *use* our religion, to put our faith into action.

As recorded in John 14:12, on the night before he died, Jesus spoke to his disciples, and to us, saying,

> *"Amen, amen, I solemnly assure you, the man who has faith in me will do the works I do, and greater far than these. Why? Because I go to the Father, and whatever you ask in my name I will do, so as to glorify the Father in the Son. Anything you ask me in my name, I will do."*

What an enormous responsibility we have, if we accept it, that is! With all of the activity and busyness in our personal lives, suffering in the lives of others, and chaos in the whole world in general, we are called to be instruments of God's healing and do even greater works than Jesus. We are called to be facilitators of restoration. What an opportunity! What a challenge!

If we stop and think about it, Jesus is calling us to nothing less than restoring peace and sanity in the world, recovering values and traditions of the past, and insisting on justice for all. We are commissioned to remind others that our tears will be turned into laughter and our mourning into dancing. And we are challenged to promote the powerfully healing virtue of hope in what sometimes may appear to be a hopeless world.

Surely, the world must have seemed hopeless to Thomas after the Crucifixion, just as it sometimes seems to us. Even though some of us can say that the pain and anguish of our personal or national crisis is abating, the signs of suffering remain.[23]

"Doubting Thomas"— John 20: 24-31

Thomas, called Didymus, one of the Twelve, was not with them when Jesus came. So the other disciples said to him, "We have seen the Lord." But he said to them, "Unless I see the mark of the nails in his hands and put my finger into the nail marks and put my hand into his side, I will not believe." Now a week later his disciples were again inside and Thomas was with them. Jesus came, although the doors were locked, and stood in their midst and said, "Peace be with you." Then he said to Thomas, "Put your finger here and see my hands, and bring your hand and put it into my side, and do not be unbelieving, but believe." Thomas answered and said to him, "My Lord and my

---

[23] Rev. Dennis Chriszt, C.P.P.S. wrote the following reflection for the *Building the Kingdom in a Changing World* parish mission. Reprinted here with permission of the author.

God!" Jesus said to him, "Have you come to believe because you have seen me? Blessed are those who have not seen and have believed."

Now Jesus did many other signs in the presence of [his] disciples that are not written in this book. But these are written that you may [come to] believe that Jesus is the Messiah, the Son of God, and that through this belief you may have life in his name.

Even after the Resurrection, Jesus continued to show signs of his suffering to Thomas. Notice that his suffering was not a limitation. Instead, it was an opportunity, as Jesus became a source of reconciliation and healing for all.

Like Jesus, we may continue to carry the signs of our suffering with us. This provides us with the opportunity to be ambassadors of reconciliation to others.

Even though the suffering had ended and new life had emerged, Jesus still bore the scars of his suffering and death. Jesus' wounds became healing wounds, scars that could bring peace and reconciliation to a situation of brokenness. Thomas' relationship with the other disciples was broken, in that he didn't trust what the disciples told him any more. His relationship with Jesus was broken, in that he didn't believe that Jesus was alive from the dead. But seeing and touching the scars on Jesus' body became the source of healing for Thomas and for the other disciples.

Our wounds may fully heal, but our healed wounds may still have scars. The pain may have fully dissipated, but the scars remind us of the suffering we endured. We may be fully-healed or not-yet-healed, but still we have reason for hope.

This gospel reading is from the end of the gospel of John. Now consider the end of the gospel of Matthew. Je-

sus tells the disciples to go forth and make disciples of all nations. He sends them out with a message of hope for the whole world. But this is not the first time he has done so. Earlier in their relationship he sent them out. He told them to take nothing with them, but to simply proclaim, "The reign of God is in your midst." Perhaps they didn't feel ready to go. Perhaps they weren't perfectly prepared, but they went anyway.

We may not yet feel completely healed or completely prepared to go out, either. We may still bear the marks of our suffering and pain. Yet Jesus sends us out, too. When he sent the disciples, he sent them two by two. He sent them empowered with the Spirit. Likewise, we are not alone. We are commissioned to go forth with others, empowered with his Spirit.

In the early Church, they called the Mass by several different names. It was known as the breaking of the bread —a time to remember that Jesus had been broken for them (and for us). It was called the Eucharist—a time to give thanks. And a little later, it was called Missa—the sending. We celebrate those very same realities.

This is a time in our history to remember the brokenness Jesus experienced for us, as we share his broken body and poured out blood. This is a time to give thanks for all that God has already done and all that God will do in and for us in the future. This is also a time to be sent. We may bear the scars of our suffering. The wounds may not be healed yet. They could still be fresh in our memory, the pain still present in our hearts, minds and souls. Nevertheless, it is time to be sent as the disciples were sent. The reign of God is in our midst, and we need to proclaim it to others.

The Paschal Mystery

Of course, we know the world is not hopeless. It just seems that way sometimes, as it may have to Thomas.

World affairs and current events can be so overwhelming at times that the future of humanity appears, at best, confusing and complicated with no clear sense of direction, or at worst, rapidly taking a course which leads to deterioration and destruction.

The truth of the matter is that Jesus is calling *us* to be facilitators of hope, and joy in spite of the confusing, complicated, and destructive course the world seems to be taking. Jesus is calling *you and me! Us!* Jesus has said that *you and I "will do these works and even greater things than these."*

The current trials we have experienced in recent major crises and in our own lives can be described quite accurately as the paschal mystery, the dying and rising, the death and the resurrection which we all experience, sometimes on a daily basis.

Since I began writing the manuscript for this book, my own family has provided dramatic examples of the dying and rising process. My son, Tommy, woke up one morning with an enormous swollen gland under his right jaw. By the end of the day, his doctor had ordered a biopsy of the very large, painless lymph gland. Of course, I immediately went to my medical journals and the Internet for information concerning "large, painless lymph glands." I found that this is the main symptom of malignant lymphoma. I was terrified, and so was Tommy, his sisters, and our whole family.

Immediately, I sent out prayer requests over the Internet to a vast circuit of prayer partners. They responded with messages of support for Tommy, which I copied and joyfully printed out for him. These messages also told of the many prayer requests that they had sent out to other prayer circles. Soon, we were receiving many, many prayers—even from remote and distant areas.

The biopsy was done the following Monday. We would have to wait eleven days to learn the results.

During these eleven long, long days, I prayed. I begged God to protect my son. I stormed Heaven but found little peace for myself as I continued to learn more and more about lymphoma.

Meanwhile, on the very same day of Tommy's biopsy, my daughter Debbie had a miscarriage. It was her first pregnancy, and she and her husband Chris were very upset. She wept. Chris wept. I wept. Tommy wept. And God wept . . . for we know that when our children weep, we weep. I'm sure it is the same for God!

Finally, on the appointed day, Tommy asked me if I would go with him to get the results from the doctor. Do you want to know what the sweetest sounding six-letter word in the world is? BENIGN! Thank you, Lord.

We had crossed one hurdle, but now we had others ahead of us. Tommy had to have several more MRI's since the first one showed more than twenty swollen glands in and around his throat area. Even though the tumor was not malignant, doctors now suspected Hodgkin's Disease, especially since there were so many nodules in Tommy's throat.

So, back I went to the Internet and learned everything I could about Hodgkin's. The stages of this disease are determined by the location of the swollen glands—Stage 1 if only in the throat area; Stage 2 if in the chest; Stage 3 or 4 if in the abdomen.

The abdominal MRI showed nothing, but more swollen lymph glands were found in the chest MRI—under Tommy's left lung and beneath his trachea. Hodgkin's was more suspicious than ever. I became more convinced than ever that Tommy was terribly ill.

For an accurate diagnosis to be made, though, Tommy had to have extensive blood work, and the hematologist would be the final diagnostician. Again, many days passed before we could get any results.

By this time, of course, I was positive that Tommy had Stage II Hodgkin's, and I was mentally preparing for a long fight with radiation and chemotherapy. With such typical symptoms of Hodgkin's and no hope in sight, I continued to pray and beg God for intervention. Even though I wanted to trust God, in all honesty, I became more and more depressed as each day went by.

One day a good friend and prayer partner of mine wrote to me to encourage me that perhaps the situation was not as bad as it seemed. *"How could that be?"* I asked myself, now an *expert* on Hodgkin's disease. All of the symptoms pointed to it, including the fact that by now, Tommy was also having night sweats. However, she told me that her young adult son had had similar symptoms several years earlier and it turned out to be nothing. *"Nothing?"* I asked myself. *"Could this possibly be true? Was there hope for Tommy?"* Yes, there was hope, and this first ray of hope gave me peace of mind for the first time in nearly two months.

Finally, the hematologist told Tommy that he was "one very fortunate young man." He said that their worst fear was Hodgkin's, but it looked like he must have had a viral infection, or, possibly mononucleosis. While it cannot be medically documented since a diagnosis of Hodgkin's was never made, I still consider it a miracle. God answered our prayers.

Another miracle was how my friend's message of hope soothed my fears, calmed my mind, and gave me hope for the first time.

Tommy now considers himself one of the most grateful people in the world and says he will "be walking around on his knees for a long time."

And Debbie just told me a week ago that she is pregnant again! The cycle—the dying and the rising—the fear and the relief—the dread and the good news—the crucifixion and the resurrection—the sorrow and the joy! My cup truly runneth over.

The Importance of Hope

As you can see, I had forgotten to hope for the best in Tommy's case, and it was not until my friend shared her story that *hope* entered my mind during this incident. This is one very practical way that we all can become facilitators of recovery, restoration, and healing. By sharing our own faith stories with others, especially when they are experiencing stress or crisis in their lives, we can reestablish the sense of hope for them which leads to healing and wholeness.

Medical research has shown the significance of the element of hope in the healing and recovery process. It sometimes is referred to as *the placebo effect*. When people are given a simple sugar pill but believe that it may be a new and powerful drug, some of them become better. In many double blind studies, where neither the subjects nor the doctors knew which patients were receiving the medication and which were receiving the placebo, substantial improvement is often seen in a significant number of subjects receiving the placebo. Little is understood about this so-called "placebo effect." It is just one indication of the mind-body connection in healing.

Hope has always been an absolutely necessary element for growth, stability, healing, recovery, and restoration. Elie Wiesel writes: "When God created us, God gave Adam a secret—and that secret was not how to begin, but how to begin again. In other words, it is not given to us to begin; that privilege is God's alone. But it is given to us to begin again—and we do every time we choose to defy death and side with the living."

Even in Greek mythology, we see the importance of hope. Pandora was the first woman on earth, created at the request of the god Zeus. She was sent to Epimetheus to be his bride although Epimetheus had been warned never to accept anything from Zeus. The gods had given her a box, warning her never to open it. Her curiosity finally overcame her, however, and she opened the mysterious box. Innumerable plagues for the body and sorrows for the mind flew out of the box. In terror, she tried to shut the box, but only Hope remained in the box. Hope was the one good thing among many evils the box had contained, and hope remained to comfort humanity in its misfortunes.

The old adage, *Where there's life, there's hope*, is often used to encourage people when it seems that there is no hope. However, I think that the opposite also is true, *Where there is hope, there is life!* The opposite of hope is hopelessness, and without hope, there is despair. Hopelessness often leads to severe depression and sometimes suicide.

The most evocative description of faith in the *New Testament* is found in *Hebrews* 11:1, where faith is heralded as "the assurance of things *hoped* for, the conviction of things not seen."

The *Catechism of the Catholic Church* defines hope as "the theological virtue by which we desire the kingdom of heaven and eternal life as our happiness, placing our trust in Christ's promises and relying not on our own strength, but on the help of the grace of the Holy Spirit.

"The virtue of hope responds to the aspiration to happiness which God has placed in every human heart; it takes up the hopes that inspire our activities and purifies them so as to order them to the Kingdom; hope keeps us from discouragement; it sustains us during times of abandonment; it opens up our hearts in expectation of eternal beatitude. The *Our Father* is the summary of everything that hope leads us to desire."[24]

---

[24] CCC, #1817-1818.

Jesus said that he came to give us life to the full, abundant life. Life cannot be abundant or "to the full" if it lacks the element of hope. The joy we know and savor would not be experienced as fully if it were not contrasted with our sadness, tears and doubts.

I have come to a point in my life where I can look back and see that the training, the experience, and the knowledge that I have gained over a lifetime is for a specific purpose. I understand that it is to be used to facilitate the healing, training, and knowledge of others. This, the cycle of dying and rising in my own life, is coming full circle. Only now am I beginning to understand the reasons, the "whys and wherefores," of many of the various pathways my life journey has included, all of which underline the power of hope.

Personal Holiness: Antidote to Powerlessness

So, we return to the questions, "How do we assist others, as well as ourselves, to transform life's pain into power? How can we focus on recovery and reconstruction? What can we do to help prevent similar problems in the future? How can we assist each other in the recovery process?"

One particular word was used frequently to describe the victims, both direct and indirect, of the three crises of terrorism, sexual abuse of minors, and corporate fraud. That word was *powerless.*

Powerless is defined in the dictionary as "weak, feeble, impotent, unable." The powerlessness that many people felt in conjunction with the terrorists, the abusive priests, and the corporate executives was of a negative variety and left many people with a sense of hopelessness and despair, which is not of God.

In a spiritual sense, however, powerlessness may generate positive benefits since it compels us to admit our own limitations. We are not God! Powerlessness, in this sense, may drive us into the arms of our loving Father. It may lead us to seek Jesus, our rock and our cornerstone.

Personal holiness can do much to provide an antidote to the negative sense of helplessness or powerlessness. St. Paul reminds us,

"You must put on the armor of God . . . Stand fast, with the truth as the belt around your waist, justice as your breastplate, and zeal to propagate the gospel of peace as your footgear. In all circumstances hold faith up before you as your shield. . . Take the helmet of salvation and the sword of the spirit, the word of God (Ephesians 6:13-17)."

Spiritual growth is facilitated by all of the elements mentioned in this passage: truth, justice, zeal, peace, faith, salvation, Scripture. There are many means to growing in our faith: frequenting the sacraments, actively participating in the local faith community, personal and communal prayer, Scripture study, retreats, veneration of the saints, alms-giving, repentance, and fasting, one of the least understood methods.

Eight Reasons to Fast

Fasting is a valid and traditional means of sincere repentance and spiritual growth. So far, little has been said about the effects of fasting as a discipline on our journey toward holiness. One of our lay preachers, Christine Watkins, provided me with a helpful list of eight reasons to fast which she uses in some of her Isaiah Mission presentations:

> 1) Fasting unites us with the poor who are the majority of the people in the world. Most people live on a simple diet of foods such as rice and beans. Most of us in the United States live in comparative luxury.

> 2) Prayer without fasting is like Christmas without Easter. Prayer without fasting is

like a bird trying to fly with one wing. If we do not offer the willing sacrifice of prayer and fasting, our spiritual growth will be severely limited. Prayer with fasting is so powerful that it can even avert war.

3) Fasting was a common practice in Jesus' time. The book of *Acts* indicates that prayer and fasting was an important element in the lives of the early members of the Church and in the growth of the Church. (See *Acts* 14:23.)

4) The Church, speaking through *The Catechism of the Catholic Church*, urges us to participate in acts of penance, including fasting. (See paragraph 1438.)

5) Prayer with fasting can bring remarkable results in intercessory prayer. If we are willing to offer the sacrifice of prayer and fasting for others, God knows that we are serious about our prayer. A version of *Mark* 9:29 describes a situation where the disciples asked Jesus why they were not able to cast out a demon from a boy. Jesus responded: "This kind can only come out through prayer and through fasting."

6) Fasting purifies our souls and leads us closer to God, if we fast with a spirit of love. When we fast, we may see certain aspects of the flesh rise up within ourselves, such as irritability, self-pity, anger, pride, or lust. It is easy to assume that the fasting is causing such reactions. In fact, the fasting enables

us to recognize these reactions as elements of the flesh within us, so that we might experience spiritual purification.

7) Fasting one day a week greatly facilitates spiritual growth. Fasting on just bread and water, especially on Fridays, seems to be an extremely efficacious type of fast. If people cannot fast from food due to health reasons, they can seek guidance from God about something else they could give up. Offering up something that we greatly desire is extremely pleasing to God.

8) Ultimately fasting is an act of the will. Our bodies may protest the fasting with temporary side-effects, such as hunger, headaches, tiredness, or stomach aches. Except for health reasons, these side-effects won't keep us from fasting. But a weak will can keep us from fasting.[25]

Spiritual Growth

Jesus Christ is the cornerstone of our lives, of our very existence. It is beneficial from time to time to assess our measure of worship, of adoration, of discipline as disciples of the Lord. Sometimes, it is helpful to examine our own spiritual growth.

    1. Do we still thirst for God as much as we did earlier in our journey?

    2. Are we increasingly governed by Scripture, by the teaching of the Church, by the wisdom of the prophets and saints?

---

[25] Contributed by Christine Self Watkins, an Isaiah lay preacher who holds a graduate degree in theology.

3. Do we celebrate the sacraments joyfully and intentionally or do we take them for granted?

4. Are we praying as much as we did earlier in our faith journey? Have we developed our prayer lives to include more forms of prayer than merely rote prayers? Do we pray in good times as well as bad? Do we talk with God very often? Do we listen enough?

5. Do we delight in the Church, the Body of Christ?

6. Are disciplines such as prayer, fasting, and almsgiving becoming more important to us?

7. Is our care for others more important to us than demonstrating our own piety?

8. Do we grieve over sin?

9. Are we growing more concerned over other's needs?

10. Do we delight in Jesus, Our Lord?

The Role of the Laity

Two laypeople, in particular, come to mind when discussing the results of personal holiness in relationship to using our gifts in the healing and restoration process.

"At various times throughout history, the Catholic Church has been in need of renewal and rebuilding. Often God raised up laypeople through whom he could bring about renewal. Two good examples are St. Francis of Assisi and St. Catherine of Siena. . . .

"St. Francis and St. Catherine were ordinary laypeople, who became extraordinary because of their obedience to Jesus' command that we *love God with our whole heart and love our neighbor as ourselves.* In this way, they had tremendous impact on the Church of their day. We, too, are called to love God with our whole heart and to love our neighbor as ourselves. If we live our lives in this way, we too can have tremendous impact on the Church of our day."[26]

We will be able to rebuild the church and the world as we respond to God's call—a call to personal holiness of the clergy and laity alike. In regard to the abuse of power crisis in the Church, one critically necessary change was suggested by Bishop Wilton Gregory, President of the United States Conference of Bishops, and was supported by most of the bishops present at their historic June 2002 meeting in Dallas. That one very necessary change for prevention of similar problems in the future was greater involvement in the Church by the laity.

One lay speaker at that Dallas meeting lamented that the "only leverage that the laity have is money—and that is a scandal in itself." Yes, that is a scandal. What can be done to change it?

Remember the cartoon where Pogo said, "I have met the enemy and they is us?" Ultimately, that may apply to lay members of the Church who are caught up in the inertia of apathy. On the other hand, many Catholic lay people may *appear* to be apathetic about their role in the Church, not because they do not care about the Church, but simply because they do not know *what* they can do, *what* they are allowed to do, *what* they are called to do, or *what* they are empowered to do.

Marching Papers

A Vatican II definition of *church* and a new understanding of the role of the laity are both necessary and enlightening components of the renewal and rebuilding of the Church. Vatican II redefined *church* as the "People of God"—*people*, not a building or an institution.

---

[26] Janice M. Valvano, "Rebuilding the Church," 2002. Please see Appendix F for the entire essay.

Cardinal Avery Dulles, S.J., wrote in his introduction to the Vatican II document known as *Lumen Gentium*, "Instead of beginning with a discussion of the structures and government of the Church, this document starts with the notion of the Church as a people to whom God communicates himself in love."[27]

The editor of the collected Vatican II documents also adds a footnote to this definition of the Church: "This title, People of God, solidly founded in Scripture, met a profound desire of the Council to put greater emphasis on the human and communal side of the Church, rather than on the institutional and hierarchical aspects which have sometimes been over stressed in the past."[28]

In the *Decree on the Apostolate of the Laity (Apostolicam Actuositatem)*, the bishops of Vatican II turned their attention to the role of the laity in the mission of the Church. In the opening paragraph, evangelization is affirmed as the primary purpose of the Church: "For this the Church was founded: that by spreading the kingdom of Christ everywhere for the glory of God the Father, she might bring all to share in Christ's saving redemption. . . . All activity directed to the attainment of this goal is called the apostolate."[29]

In that same paragraph, the bishops state in no uncertain terms that the laity has a special and indispensable role in this apostolate. "No member is passive . . . and the member who fails to make his proper contribution to the development of the Church must be said to *be useful neither to the Church nor to himself*."[30]

Then the bishops wrote, "On all Christians therefore is laid the *splendid burden* of working to make the divine

---

[27] Walter M. Abbott, S.J., Ed., *The Documents of Vatican II*. Chicago: Follett, 1966, p.12.
[28] Ibid., p. 24.
[29] *Apostolicam Actuositatem*, 2.
[30] Ibid. (emphasis mine.)

message of salvation known and accepted by all men throughout the world."[31] (Many lay people mark this statement by the 2500 bishops gathered in Rome as giving the lay people their marching orders.)

Role of the Laity Updated

In 1980 the United States bishops addressed the whole Church but focused specifically on the laity in their document, *"Called and Gifted."* In it the bishops acknowledged and reflected upon the ways lay men and women were answering the Lord's call and employing their gifts to take an active and responsible part in the mission of the Church. Fifteen years later, in their 1995 document, *"Called and Gifted for the Third Millennium,"* the U.S. bishops reaffirmed the four "calls" of the laity in the original document—to holiness, to community, to mission and ministry, and to adulthood/Christian maturity.

"During the last fifteen years," the bishops wrote, "the Christian lay faithful have contributed greatly to the spiritual heritage of the Church, enlarging our understanding of what it means to be called to holiness, that is to be called to 'ever more intimate union with Christ' (*Catechism of the Catholic Church*, No. 2014). Their union with Christ is evident in a deepened awareness of the spiritual dimensions of life."

However, the bishops were quick to add, ". . . 'spiritual sight' or insight is not sufficient in itself. The call to holiness requires effort and commitment to live the beatitudes. . . . The laity's call to holiness is a gift from the Holy Spirit. Their response is a gift to the Church and to the world."

Mutual Ministry

Let's agree to pray and fast that the laity will become more involved, more concerned, and more mutually

---

[31] Ibid. 3 (emphasis mine.)

engaged in ministry. Let us pray the dream of Vatican II will be fulfilled: that the laity *alongside* of the clergy and hierarchy will become ministers of reconciliation and healing united—not in competition with each other.

Clergy and laity are mutually gifted, although not necessarily with the same gifts, and have an equal responsibility to obey Jesus' command, *"Love one another as I have loved you."*

In an article in the *Boston Globe* entitled "A Crisis of Clergy, Not of Faith," in March 2002, well before the bishops met in Dallas in June, Lisa Sowle Cahill, a professor of theology and ethics at Boston College wrote, "Fortunately, the Roman Catholic Church is more than its bureaucracy. There are many priests and pastors, and even some bishops, who share the bewilderment and anger of their congregations and are struggling with them for justice and reconciliation. And there is the strength of the laity itself. . . .

"Far-reaching reform can only take place when lay people have a more powerful voice in church decisions, on both the local and national levels. This does not necessarily mean that they must organize in opposition to their pastors, for many priests are allies in this struggle. It is merely to say that lasting institutional change will require the equal participation of the laity, priests, bishops, and the Vatican itself.

"This crisis may mobilize Catholics to demand a greater role in the church, and in doing so they may strengthen its moral authority and enlarge its sense of responsibility. Better yet, it may help them to realize that the future of any religious tradition, no matter how ancient, is in the hands of all its believers."

What Do We Do Now?

1. We pray for each other.
2. We feel each other's pain.

3. We share our "happy ending" stories of hope.
4. We share our "sad ending" stories of suffering.
5. We transform our stumbling blocks for healing into stepping stones.
6. We recognize the mystery of faith, the paschal mystery of dying and rising, in our own lives.
7. We welcome the opportunity for growth along with the suffering in each crisis we face.
8. We pray for peace and work for justice.
9. We invite resilience in each other, to begin again.
10. We walk with each other and support each other in all ways.

Invite others to get involved in making positive changes in our Church and in our world. Show them the importance of prayer, fasting, justice issues, and lay participation in leadership. Challenge your friends, support your clergy, and unite all.

Encourage everyone to develop a personal love relationship with Jesus, who leads us to the Father, through the action of the Holy Spirit. When we have that personal love relationship with Jesus, then we can reach out to others with the genuine love that comes from God. Loving others is not an option for Christians. It's a commandment. Do not be afraid to get involved or act on your faith "For God did not give us a spirit of cowardice but rather of power and love and self-control" (2 *Timothy* 1:7).

Challenge people to have the courage to be peacemakers, to take the time to perform random acts of kindness in their daily lives, to make this a "kinder and gentler" world. What are we doing for the poor? How are we welcoming Arab-American/Cuban/Mexican/Asian families in our neighborhoods, schools, workplaces, church? Are we praying for peace in the face of threats of nuclear war? How do we react to prejudicial slurs or jokes? What is our legacy to our children and grandchildren, to all future generations? Are we living the *Beatitudes*?

Sharing the Eucharist can be a first step as we celebrate that God walks with us throughout the process of reconciliation. We are not alone. We are reminded in the Road to Emmaus story (*Luke* 24:13-35) that God walks with us even at times when we think he has abandoned us. In *Matthew* 28:20, God tells us clearly *"And know that I am with you even to the end of the world."* And most importantly, *the bottom line* comes from *John* 16:33: *"I tell you all this that, in me you may find peace. You will suffer in the world. But take courage. I have overcome the world."*

Yes, we are sent to facilitate recovery, restoration, and hope for the Kingdom of God in a Changing World. With the myriad of gifts we each possess and with a new commitment to personal holiness, we are to be instruments of change. The Good News is that God goes with us. We are not alone!

Updated Beatitudes

The pastor of St. Stephen Church in Winter Springs, Florida, Father John J. Bluett, shared contrasting sets of updated versions of the beatitudes in a homily which was published in the *Florida Catholic*.[32] Perhaps more than anything else I have seen or read, these words define the differences between our pre-September 11 world and our post-September 11 world.

Pre-September 11 Version of the Beatitudes

The first version was written by Joan Demerchant. "Let's face it," she wrote. "If the beatitudes were written to accurately reflect the predominant values of 21st Century America, they might read:

---

[32] Father John J. Bluett, "Have the beatitudes gone stale for us?" Florida Catholic, February 7, 2002, page 15.

Blessed are the powerful, for they shall control others.
Blessed are the movers and shakers, for they shall make things happen.
Blessed are the strong, the young, and the beautiful, for they shall be greatly admired.
Blessed are those of white, European descent, for they shall inherit the earth.
Blessed are the winners, for they shall be praised and applauded.
Blessed are the affluent, for they shall have what they need and also everything that they want.
Blessed are Americans, for they shall live in God's one and only beloved country.
Blessed are those in authority, for they shall possess all power and truth.

Father Bluett then comments, "These words would have been hard to challenge (prior to September 11). Our heroes were Enron CEOs and dot-com billionaires, film stars, and sports giants. Suddenly our heroes became firefighters and police officers, members of our military, and ordinary passengers on an airplane.

"Then I thought: This is just what Jesus did when he turned everything upside-down when he sat down and talked to the people all those centuries ago. The people had thought that God blessed the rich and the healthy and the powerful above all others. That brings me to another updated version of the beatitudes:

Post-September 11 Version of the Beatitudes
If you're struggling to pay the bills, but insist on making time to be with your children whenever they need you, **blessed are you—you may never own the big vacation home and the fanciest car, but heaven will be yours.**

If you are overwhelmed by the care of a dying spouse, a sick child, or an elderly parent, but you are determined to spend precious time easing their journey for them, **blessed are you—one day your sorrow will be transformed into joy.**

If you willingly give your time to cook at a soup kitchen, vacuum the church, or help in a classroom; if you befriend the uncool, the unpopular, the perpetually lost, **blessed are you—count God among your friends and biggest boosters.**

If you refuse to take shortcuts when it comes to doing what is right, if you refuse to compromise your integrity and ethics, if you refuse to take refuge in the rationalization that 'everybody does it,' **blessed are you—you will triumph.**

If you try to understand things from the perspective of the other person, and you always manage to find a way to make things work for the good; if you are feeling discouraged and frustrated because you are always worrying, always waiting, always bending over backward, always paying the price for loving the unlovable and forgiving the undeserving, **blessed are you—God will welcome, forgive and love you.**

If you struggle to discover what God asks of you in all things; if you seek God's presence in every facet of your life and every decision you make; if your constant prayer is not 'give me' but rather 'help me,' **blessed are you—God will always be there for you.**

If you readily spend time listening and consoling anyone who looks to you for support, for guidance, for compassion; if you manage to heal the wounds and build bridges; if others see in you graciousness, joy and serenity; if you can see the good in everyone and seek the good for everyone, **blessed are you— you are nothing less than God's own.**

If you are rejected or demeaned because of the color of your skin, or your accent, or the sound of your name; if your faith in what is holy, by whatever name you call it, automatically puts you at odds with some people; if you refuse to compromise to 'get along' or 'not make waves,' **blessed are you— one day you will live with God.**

Closing Prayer
Prayer of St. Francis

Lord, make me an instrument of thy peace.
Where there is hatred, let me sow love;
Where there is injury, pardon;
Where there is discord, union;
Where there is doubt, faith;
Where there is despair, hope;
Where there is darkness, light,
Where there is sadness, joy.

Oh Divine Master, grant that I may not so
much seek to be consoled as to console,
To be understood as to understand,
To be loved as to love.

For it is in giving that we receive,
It is in pardoning that we are pardoned,
And it is in dying that we are born to eternal life.

Food for Thought

Micah 6:8:
"Only three things are required of you:
to live justly, to love mercy,
and to walk humbly with our God."

Practical Suggestions:

1. Identify your own greatest need in terms of growing in holiness.

2. Research or create opportunities for lay involvement in the Church, in your diocese, in your own parish.

3. Explore and define your responsibility as a layperson in the church. Are you caught up in the old "pay, pray, and obey" mindset? If so, take the first steps to change into a layperson who is accountable in terms of initiative, generosity, and service.

4. Consider ways that you can be "not just *hearers*, but *doers* of the Word."

5. Think of ways that injustice creeps into your own life or neighborhood. Are there poor, homeless, hopeless present? Ask yourself what you can do to prevent these situations.

6. Can you identify any ways in which you might be racist, prejudiced, biased? Begin to work on changing this in your own life.

7. Sponsor a child or elderly person in the Third World:
Christian Foundation for Children and Aging
One Elmwood Avenue
Kansas City, Kansas 66103
800-875-6564
E-mail: mail@cfcausa.org
Web site: www.cfcausa.org

Prayerful Suggestions:

1. Use the list you made of all the things that you are grateful for as a prayer tool. Thank God for each and every item on your list.

2. Pray that God will help us now and that God's presence will be revealed to you and others. Pray to see/realize the reality of God's presence.

3. Set aside daily prayer time to ask for God's peace, protection, and presence for you, your family, your community, your country, the world.

4. Utilize on a daily basis the unique gifts and charisms that God has given you to help restore peace in the world and in your neighborhood.

5. Pray and fast for peace and justice in the world.

6. Attend Mass frequently offering your intentions for world peace, stability.

7. Continue to pray for our nation's 46,000 dedicated priests and our 63 million laity. Our Church depends on all of us, clergy and lay.

8. In your prayer and in your life, always focus on what Jesus would do.

For Reflection/Discussion

1. What opportunities are there for lay leadership or lay formation in your parish or diocese? Is lay ministry training available to you? If so, would you participate in it? Why? Why not?

2. Think of times in your own life when opportunities arose which gave you opportunities to be a peacemaker. What were the circumstances? What happened?

3. In light of some of the painful circumstances in your life or in your community that have been discussed in the past few weeks, what concrete steps can you take toward resolution?

4. What have you learned about yourself or about your faith community in the past few weeks of participating in this course?

Gaelic Blessing

Deep peace of the running wave to you,
Deep peace of the flowing air to you,
Deep peace of the quiet earth to you,
Deep peace of the shining stars to you,
Deep peace of the gentle night to you,
Moon and stars pour their healing light on you,
Deep peace of Christ, the light of the world, to you,
Deep peace of Christ to you.

Growth in Holiness
I Peter 2:1 – 7

So strip away everything vicious, everything deceitful; pretenses, jealousies, and disparaging remarks of any kind.

Be as eager for milk as newborn babies—pure milk of the spirit to make you grow unto salvation, now that you have tasted that the LORD is good.

Come to him, a living stone, rejected by men but approved, nonetheless and precious in God's eyes. You too are living stones, built as an edifice of spirit, into a holy priesthood, offering spiritual sacrifices acceptable to God through Jesus Christ. For Scripture has it:

"See, I am laying a stone in Zion, a stone that has been tested, a precious cornerstone as a sure foundation; he who puts faith in it shall not be shaken" (Is. 28:16).

The stone is of value for you who have faith. For those without faith, it is rather,

"A stone which the builders rejected that became a cornerstone" (Rom. 9: 33).

Appendix A

REVISED HOLMES RAHE SOCIAL READJUSTMENT SCALES[33]
Scale for Adults (18 and over)

Life Event   **Life Change Units**
Death of A Spouse 100
Divorce 73
Marital Separation 65
Imprisonment 63
Death of a Close Family Member 63
Personal Injury or Illness 53
Marriage 50
Dismissal from Work 47
Marital Reconciliation 45
Retirement 45
Change in Health of Family Member 44
Pregnancy 40
Sexual Difficulties 39
Gain a New Family Member 39
Business Readjustment 39
Change in Financial State 38
Change in Frequency of Arguments 35
Major Mortgage 32
Foreclosure of Mortgage or Loan 30
Change in Responsibilities at Work 29
Child Leaving Home 29

---

[33] Ellen A. Mogensen, "The Holmes-Rahe Social Readjustment Scales," http://www.healpastlives.com/future/cure/scale.htm, October 17, 2002.

Trouble with In-Laws 29
Outstanding Personal Achievement 28
Spouse Starts or Stops Work 26
Begin or End School 26
Change in Living Conditions 25
Revision of Personal Habits 24
Trouble with Boss 23
Change in Working Hours or Conditions 20
Change in Residence 20
Change in Schools 20
Change in Recreation 19
Change in Church Activities 19
Change in Social Activities 18
Minor Mortgage or Loan 17
Change in Sleeping Habits 16
Change in Number of Family Reunions 15
Change in Eating Habits 15
Vacation 13
Christmas 12
Minor Violation of Law 11

Scoring:
300+: Be extremely careful. You are at a greatly increased risk of serious illness (reduce stress now!)

150-299: Be cautious. Your risk of illness is moderate (reduced by 30% from the above risk).

150 or less: Be glad. You only have a slight risk of illness (but still need to take care of yourself!)

Scale for Children (18 and under)
Getting Married 100
Unwed pregnancy 92
Death of Parent 87
Acquiring a Visible Deformity 81

Divorce of parents 77
Fathering an unwed pregnancy 77
Becoming involved with drugs/alcohol 76
Jail sentence of parent for over 1 year 75
Marital separation of parents 69
Death of a brother or sister 68
Change in acceptance by peers 67
Pregnancy of unwed sister 64
Discovery of being an adopted child 63
Marriage of parent to step-parent 63
Death of a close friend 63
Having a visible congenital deformity 62
Serious illness requiring hospitalization 58
Failure of a grade in school 56
Not making an extracurricular activity 55
Hospitalization of a parent 55
Jail sentence of parent for over 30 days 53
Breaking up with boyfriend or girlfriend 53
Beginning to date 51
Suspension from school 50
Birth of a brother or sister 50
Increase of arguments between parents 47
Loss of job by parent 46
Outstanding personal achievement 46
Change in parent's financial status 45
Accepted at a college of your choice 43
Being a senior in high school 42
Hospitalization of a sibling 41
Increased absence of parent from home 38
Brother or sister leaving home 37
Addition of third adult to family 34
Becoming a full fledged member of a church 31

Scoring: Same as above.

Appendix B

FACILITATOR'S GUIDE

Weekly Meetings

Each week a chapter should be assigned to be read in advance and the reflection questions completed. Then for each meeting, the format is fairly standard:

Opening Prayer
Appropriate Scripture Reading
Brief overview of the content of each chapter
(by a different volunteer each week)
General discussion
(Based on the participants' prayerful reflections
of the material at the end of the chapter.)
*Closing Prayer
Fellowship

*Note: When using this manual for
pre-mission spiritual preparation, add:
Update of Preparation for the Mission
(For Weeks 1, 2, 4, 5)
Third Week – CFCA Presentation

A short period of fellowship with simple refreshments, if possible, after each meeting is encouraged so that people can get to know each other better and perhaps share more personally with one another. In either case, of using this manual as a resource for either pre-or-post mission use, the meetings should not run more than an hour and a half.

Appendix C

COMMON REACTIONS TO STRESSFUL EVENTS

Psychologists recognize that all individuals do not react to stress in the same way physiologically. A generalized list suggesting some of the more or less standard physical reactions to stressful events are as follows:
1. Rapid beating of the heart
2. Perspiration (mostly of the palms)
3. A rise in blood pressure
4. Dilation of the pupils
5. Stomach seems to "knot up"
6. Difficulty in swallowing (a "lump in the throat")
7. "Tight" feeling in the chest

All of these physiological symptoms mean that the organism is gearing up for a response to a stressor. This phenomenon is known as the "fight or flight" response and was first described in the 1920s by Walter B. Cannon, a Harvard University Professor of Physiology.

Is Stress Always Bad For You?

Distress, defined as excessive levels of continued, damaging stress, always has the potential of being harmful. However, stress, in and of itself, is a normal instinctual reaction of protection, alerting us to deploy corrective measures against emotional or physical pressure or, in extreme situations, to protect us from danger. Stress is the body's alarm system and is the way we feel under pressure. The pressure can be internal or external, real or imagined, but in a sense it alerts us to the fact something is wrong, like a fever alerts us to the presence of infection.

A little bit of stress is normal and good for us. It is what motivates us to push ourselves to do well in life, to run the extra mile, to count calories, to pass the test, to produce a superior report. Some people work much better under stress, and the stress of deadlines, for instance, becomes a positive motivator. (Absolutely no stress would indicate that you are no longer alive.)

However, too much stress inhibits enjoyment of our lives. For example, we feel too much pressure to get that promotion, to complete graduate work, or to make financial ends meet. Stressful situations over which we have no control cause the most frustration, as we unsuccessfully search for solutions through trial and error. We get very upset, life isn't very much fun anymore, and we cannot see the light at the end of the tunnel. This is stress overload—a situation in which stress has turned into distress and can be damaging.

SIGNS OF STRESS OVERLOAD

Like an overloaded computer, "stress overload" also may result in a crash, a breakdown of the human nervous system. This is the classic beginning of the third stage of stress, exhaustion.

Common signs of being stressed out include:
1. Feeling depressed, edgy, guilty, tired
2. Having headaches, stomachaches, trouble sleeping
3. Laughing or crying for no reason
4. Blaming other people for bad things that happen to you
5. Only seeing the down side of a situation
6. Feeling like things that you used to enjoy aren't fun anymore or are a burden
7. Resenting other people or your responsibilities.

Appendix D

REACTIONS TO SEVERE CRISIS[34]

Physical Reactions:
1. Fatigue/exhaustion
2. Sleep disturbance
3. Underactivity/overactivity
4. Change in appetite
5. Digestive problems
6. Nightmares
7. Muscle tremors/twitches
8. Startle reactions
9. Headaches
10. Dizziness
11. Muscle aches
12. Vomiting

Cognitive Reactions:
1. Difficulty concentrating
2. Difficulty solving problems
3. Flashbacks of the event
4. Difficulty in making decisions
5. Memory disturbance
6. Isolation/withdrawal
7. Preoccupation with the event
8. Lowered attention span
9. Slower thinking
10. Problems naming familiar objects/people

Emotional Reactions:
1. Guilt

---

[34] "Crisis Stress Reactions," http://www.counseling.swt.edu/crisis.htm, updated January 30, 02.

2. Feelings of helplessness
3. Emotional numbing
4. Overly sensitive
5. Amnesia for the event
6. Fear/anxiety
7. Self-doubt
8. Hyper vigilance
9. Moodiness
10. Anger which may be manifested by:
    a. Scapegoating
    b. Irritability
    c. Frustration with bureaucracy
    d. Violent fantasies

Depression: People sometimes experience a period of mild to moderate depression following exposure to a stressful event or tragic loss. Symptoms of depression include:
1. Loss/gain in weight
2. Insomnia
3. Lethargy/low energy
4. Social withdrawal, loss of sexual drive
5. Difficult concentrating
6. Persistent sad mood
7. Isolation
8. Intrusive thoughts

Remember, these are normal reactions to stress, but if any combination of these symptoms persists, consult your personal physician or a mental health professional.

Appendix E

ACUTE TRAUMA REACTION[35]

Post-traumatic stress symptoms may include:
1. A fundamental fear for the safety of your family and loved ones
2. Feelings of helplessness, powerlessness, vulnerability and deep grief
3. Recurring, persistent and painful re-experiencing of the event through dreams (nightmares) or while awake (flashbacks)
4. Emotional numbness (an inability to feel or express emotions toward family, friends, and loved ones)
5. Avoiding any reminders of the event
6. Being easily angered or aroused, on edge, easily startled (hyper arousal)
7. Becoming afraid of everything
8. Not leaving the house, or isolating yourself physically or emotionally
9. Stopping usual function, no longer maintaining daily routines
10. Survivor guilt— "Why did I survive? I should have done something more." "If only . . . "
11. Tremendous sense of loss
12. Reluctance to express your feelings
13. Losing a sense of control over your life

Trauma: Do's and Don'ts[36]
1. DO have someone stay with you for at least a few hours after a critical incident.

---

[35] "Coping with Terrorism," op. cit.
[36] This list is taken directly from McGrath, "Life Lessons", *Psychology Today*, www.psychologytoday.com/trauma, 2001.

2. DO get some periods of physical exercise, alternated with relaxation. Physical activity of any kind helps alleviate stress.
3. DO structure your time. Keep busy.
4. DO talk to people. Talk is often the most healing medicine.
5. DO reach out to others. People do care.
6. DO maintain as normal a schedule as possible.
7. DO spend time in the company of others.
8. DO help family, friends, and coworkers as much as possible by checking out how they are doing.
9. DO give yourself permission to feel rotten and share your feelings with others.
10. DO keep a journal. Write your way through sleepless hours.
11. DO realize that those around you are under stress, too.
12. DO make as many daily decisions as possible.
13. DO get plenty of rest.
14. DO eat well-balanced and regular meals—even if you don't feel like it.
15. DO be alert for signs that you may need help coping, such as becoming teary all the time.

DON'T

1. DON'T label yourself crazy. It is completely normal to experience emotional aftershocks for weeks and even months after a shattering event. Concentration is often difficult.
2. DON'T try to fight recurring thoughts, dreams or flashbacks. They are normal and will decrease over time.
3. DON'T try to hide or ignore your emotions. Although at first traumatic events typically create shock and numbness or a sense of disconnection, they give rise to unusually strong emotional reactions that last long after

the event. It is only after feelings return that you can begin to heal.
4. DON'T tell people they are "lucky it wasn't worse." Traumatized people are not consoled by such statements. Instead tell them that you are sorry such an event has occurred and you want to understand and assist them.
5. DON'T take the irritability or anger of mates or of other people personally. Everyone reacts differently to an overwhelming event. Feelings often become intense and unpredictable.
6. DON'T compare yourself with others. Everyone has different internal and external coping resources. Some people respond immediately; others have delayed reactions. And reactions can change over time.
7. DON'T withdraw. Spend time with others. Talking to others is very healing for most people.
8. DON'T make any big life changes at this time, because actions such as changing jobs tend to be highly stressful in themselves.
9. DON'T use drugs or alcohol as coping mechanisms. They only numb the pain and delay recovery.

Appendix F
REBUILDING THE CHURCH[37]

At various times throughout history, the Catholic Church has been in need of renewal and rebuilding. Today is one of those times! In this article, I address the Church's current need for renewal and rebuilding, and *our part* in bringing about renewal. Before we consider the present, let's peek into the past to see how God dealt then with the need for renewal and rebuilding.

In times past, God often raised up laypeople and gave them a passionate desire to help bring about renewal. Two good examples are St. Francis of Assisi and St. Catherine of Siena. While praying, St. Francis heard the voice of Jesus saying three times, "Francis, go and repair my house, which you see is falling down." Francis thought Jesus meant to rebuild the church building. Later, he realized that he was supposed to rebuild the Church. Francis gained the respect of Church leaders because of his personal holiness. He and his followers impacted the Church for the better through their hard work and their pure and holy lives.

St. Catherine of Siena also impacted the Church through her hard work and her holy life. God worked through her as she urged the Pope in Avignon to return the papacy to Rome, which he did. However, schism and scandal continued to plague the Church. Catherine worked tirelessly, sending hundreds of letters to Church clergy and to government officials, seeking peace and unity within the Church. Also, Catherine was a great evangelist, leading many to conversion and repentance. And she ministered to the people with hands-on kindness, such as nursing the sick.

---

[37] Janice M. Valvano, "Rebuilding the Church," 2002.

St. Francis and St. Catherine were ordinary laypeople, who became extraordinary because of their obedience to Jesus' command that we love God with our whole heart and love our neighbor as ourselves. In this way, they had tremendous impact on the Church of their day. We, too, are called to love God with our whole heart and to love our neighbor as ourselves. If we live our lives in this way, we too can have tremendous impact on the Church of our day.

Call to Personal Holiness

This is not easy. Even St. Francis and St. Catherine committed sin. We are all sinners. But, we are sinners *called to personal holiness*. We cannot excuse the sin in our own lives or the lives of others. We must hold ourselves and others accountable for sin. For example, recall the story of the Woman Caught in Adultery (John 8:1-11). After her accusers left, Jesus said, "Neither do I condemn you. Go, and from now on do not sin anymore." Jesus called her action a sin. But apparently, he didn't want her to stay there; he wanted her to go on with her life, a life unencumbered by sin. He wanted her to experience the conversion that results from true repentance.

We must move into repentance and, if possible, lead others into repentance. This is a process, not to be skipped over lightly. Repentance frees us to move into a future where we sin less and less, if at all. We need to move into a future where we are appalled at the prospect of hurting God, ourselves, and others through our sinfulness. We need to move into a future where each one of us is intent upon becoming more and more like Jesus, that is, more and more God-like. With God's grace, clergy and laity alike can become a holy People of God, forming a holy Church.

Jesus is coming back to a holy Church, his Bride, without spot or wrinkle. Currently, the Church has multiple spots and wrinkles. In his love and mercy, Jesus will not leave us in this condition. So God has allowed the sin within the Church to come to light. In this way, God is cleansing the Church. Perhaps we are experiencing what St. Peter referred to as a time of judgment.

For it is time for the judgment to begin with the household of God; if it begins with us, how will it end for those who fail to obey the gospel of God? (1 Peter 4:17 NAB)

God is cleansing us individually and collectively. This is a painful but necessary reality. Without this purification, the Church might crumble under the weight of our own sin and scandal. However, God *is* cleansing the Church, thereby saving us from ruin; for Jesus promised that he would build his Church and the gates of hell would not prevail against it. (See Matthew 16:18.)

Sin and scandal in the Church have damaged her reputation, and rightly so. But I am not as concerned about the reputation of the Church as I am concerned about the holiness of the Church.

*... Christ loved the church and handed himself over for her to **sanctify** her, **cleansing** her by the bath of water with the word, that he might present to himself the church in splendor, without spot or wrinkle or any such thing, that she might be **holy** and without blemish. (Ephesians 5:25b-27 NAB, emphasis mine)*

We will grow in personal *holiness*, if we develop an ever-deepening personal *love* relationship with Jesus, who leads us to his Father, through the action of the Holy Spirit. God is holy; God is love. So, genuine love comes from God, through us, to others. We rebuild through love. Jesus told us, "This is my commandment: love one another as I love you." (See John 15:12.) We are commanded to love, yet we cannot produce genuine love by our own strength. We must have total dependency on God to enable us to love with the true love that comes from God.

Scandal and Anger

St. Francis and St. Catherine exhibited a profound love for the Church. However, it would not surprise me if they felt some anger at the evil and injustices they saw in their day. It would be natural for us to feel some anger at the evil and injustices we see in our day. We may feel angry about losses we have experienced in the Church: loss of reputation, the loss of perceived holiness and perceived trustworthiness. Unfortunately, we know now that some members of the clergy were not as holy or as trustworthy as we wanted to believe. That hurts! That is a great loss!

Anger is a normal reaction to a loss. There are three kinds of anger: *rage, resentment* and *righteous indignation.* We can feel all three forms of anger in various levels of intensity, from mild (feeling irritated) to intense (feeling furious). Rage and resentment are destructive forms of anger. Rage lashes out to hurt others. Resentment seethes within to hurt ourselves. Rage and resentment are bad forms of anger, not because they are anger, but because they are *destructive.* On the other hand, righteous indignation is a good form of anger because it is *constructive.* There is an energy that is generated within us through anger. Righteous indignation uses that energy to motivate us to make the changes that are necessary to correct the wrong. Here's the difference. Rage and resentment attack people. Righteous indignation attacks the wrong.

Remember that there is no sin in anger. Jesus was intensely angry at times, yet the Scriptures assure us that Jesus never sinned. All four gospels relate the story of Jesus throwing the moneychangers out of the temple. Jesus' anger was intense! He felt furious! However, he used his free will to choose how he would respond to his intense anger. He chose to respond to his anger by attacking the wrong. Jesus' anger was directed at the misuse of the Temple, his Father's house. By throwing out the moneychangers, Jesus corrected the wrong. Therefore, the Cleansing of the Temple is an example of intense righteous indignation. Intense righteous indignation *feels* the same as intense rage or intense resentment. We identify the three forms of anger, not by the intensity of feeling, but by how we choose to respond to the anger.

At times, we are *supposed* to be angry. Ephesians 4:26a instructs us, "Be angry but do not sin...." Anger is not the problem; it is how we choose to express the anger. If we express our anger through rage or resentment, which attacks others or ourselves, then we may sin. If we express our anger through righteous indignation, which attacks the wrong, then we do not sin.

If we respond to scandal in the Church with rage or resentment, then that is destructive to the Church and to our relationship with the Church. On the other hand, it is constructive and highly appropriate to respond with righteous indignation. Serious wrongs have been committed that we cannot ignore. Instead, we can channel the energy of our anger into efforts to correct the wrong. We can support the new policies of the hierarchy which are designed to protect the innocent and to hold accountable the guilty. And when we see the Spirit at work in the Church, we can join in what God is doing in cleansing and renewing the Church. We can intercede for our priests, deacons, laymen and laywomen, praying for holiness within the whole Church. We can become more involved in our local parishes, asking for and attending programs facilitating spiritual growth by deepening our love relationship with God and others.

Rebuilding: Not An Easy Task

God has a *vision* of what the Church could be and should be. Pray that God will reveal to each one the part that we could play and should play in rebuilding the Church. Rebuilding the Church is not an easy task. When the voice of Jesus asked St. Francis to repair God's house, St. Francis first thought it meant rebuilding the building. It took a long time for St. Francis to realize the magnitude of what Jesus was really asking of him. It will take some time for us to perceive how we are to cooperate with the Spirit in rebuilding the Church. It will happen through the Cross.

In God's scheme of things, the Cross always leads to Resurrection. However, we cannot rush the Cross. If there must be a death, we want it to be a quick and easy death, not long agonizing hours nailed to a cross. And we want the Resurrection to be immediate, not three long cold days in a dark tomb. The Cross represents painful reality. We may be tempted to *ignore* the Cross in our efforts to mask the pain. We may want to busy ourselves in *action* in our efforts to mask the pain. But we can't skip over the Cross to get to the Resurrection. The Cross takes *time*.

Guided by the Holy Spirit, we have work to do. We must *take the time* to get in touch with our own hearts and the heart of God. It helps if we allow ourselves to name the pain inside and to feel the feelings. Gradually, we move through our feelings to acceptance of our current reality. But we don't stop there. Our vision for the future of our Church insists that things could be better. Clergy and laity alike could be holier and should be holier. Let's search our own hearts and seek the heart of God. Let's *find the time* for praying more, reading the Bible more, and growing closer to God. And then, as we grow in holiness, like St. Francis and St. Catherine, each one of us can impact our Church and our world for the better. As we respond to God's grace, let's become that Bride without spot or wrinkle. Amen! Come, Lord Jesus!

Appendix G
Group Guidelines for Discussions

1. I recognize that everyone comes to this experience with very different backgrounds, experiences, and views. I commit to **honoring differences,** knowing they add to the richness of the group's experience.

2. I will **listen intently** in order to fully understand different points of view.

3. I will always **listen respectfully** (i.e., no side conversations, no interruptions).

4. I will **respectfully seek clarification** of other perspectives to add to my understanding. If I choose to debate or disagree with a perspective that is different from mine, I will do this respectfully and lovingly.

5. I commit to assuring that **everyone has an opportunity to speak** and encourage others to speak before I speak again.

6. I will **participate fully** and share in the responsibility for the group's process and experience.

7. I agree that everything shared in this room is **totally confidential** and is not to be shared with anyone else outside of this room.